Bootleg

Damon Wayans

Bootleg

with David Asbery

HarperCollins*Publishers*

HarperCollins books may be purchased for educational, business, or sales promotional use. For information please write: Special Markets Department, HarperCollins Publishers, Inc., 10 East 53rd Street, New York, NY 10022.

FIRST EDITION

Designed by Nancy B. Field

Library of Congress Cataloging-in-Publication Data

Wayans, Damon
    Bootleg / Damon Wayans.
       p. cm.
   ISBN 0-06-019366-2
   1. Family Humor. 2. Afro-American families Humor.
  I. Title.
  PN6231.F3W39 1999
  818' .5407—dc21   99-25437

---

99 00 01 02 03 ❖ / RRD 10 9 8 7 6 5 4 3 2 1

It's easy to create a great joke.
It's harder to create great joke tellers.
This book is dedicated to my parents,
Howell and Elvira Wayans, who did it ten times.
They probably laughed a lot during sex.

Contents

Part 1

The Cult of Personality

Canceled!

I was very sad to see my brother's show get canceled because out of the three black talk shows—Keenen's, Sinbad's, and Magic's—I think that Keenen had the best one. At least he was good looking, articulate, and occasionally funny. Sinbad is a good friend of mine, and I love him, but, I just think he's too yellow to be on TV. I never had to use the hue button before on my remote control until he showed up in late night. The first time I watched the show I said to my wife, "Is something wrong with my hue? My tint must be off. Is the brotha supposed to be pink with freckles? And the damn contrast must be broken' 'cause I can't believe that he's wearing a purple, red, and green outfit."

Sinbad should have fired everyone in the wardrobe department. One time he came out with balloon pants, a tuxedo jacket, and sneakers. Even Prince used to laugh at the way Sinbad dressed. And another thing, Sinbad thought "talk show" meant he's supposed to talk during the whole damn show. Have you ever watched Sinbad do an interview? He asks a question and then answers it. All the guest can do is shake his head.

Sinbad goes off like, "Man, I saw you in your

last movie. You was good, too, and, man, you had that pretty girl. What's that pretty girl's name? 'Cause I worked with a pretty girl that looked like that pretty girl, she had big breasts—*Plow!*—and butt all over the room, HA HA HA. She was fine, too, but hey, do you do your own stunts? 'Cause I know somebody that did that, fell down, broke his back, he ain't worked since. They replaced him with two midgets, HA HA HA. Man, I would never do my own stunts, 'cause I ain't gettin' any younger and neither is this interview. Listen, we out of time. Why don't you come back and do the show again?"

"Uh, yeah I . . ." the guest would try to answer.

Sinbad would flap his arms, saying, "I'm sure you can. Everyone give him a hand. Up next a funky fresh fella from Philly that never fakes the funk. He's the original funk master funkateer, Bootsy Collins."

Then, there was Magic. Who the hell told Magic that he should do a talk show? Anybody that says "bassetball," repeated says "bassetball," doesn't have any business doing a talk show. I'm sure that sometime in his life someone tried to correct him. When he was a little boy his mom must've tried.

Magic's Mother: Hey, Earvin, what are you going to be when you grow up?
Magic: I wanna blay BASSETBALL.
Magic's Mother: Now, Earvin, it's called BAS-KET-BALL. BASKETBALL.
Magic: That's what I said, BASSETBALL. BASSETBALL, BAS-SETBALL.

Magic's Mother: Well, baby, I hope you can play it 'cause you sure can't say it.

Magic went through college. He was in the NBA. Someone had to sit him down and try to make him say it correctly. I'm sure when he was with the LA Lakers Coach Pat Riley must have pulled him aside.

Riley: Magic, if you're gonna represent the game you have to say it the right way. It's called BASKETBALL. BAS-KET-BALL. Now you try.
Magic: BASSETBALL. BAS-SET-BALL. Danks, Toach!
Riley: Ah, yeah, well, I'm glad you can play it 'cause you sure can't say it. That's enough practice for today. Tomorrow we'll work on saying "coach."

I was actually sad to see his show get canceled because it gave me a lot of laughs, most of them for the wrong reasons. But I'll take comedy any way I can get it. I wanted to be on his show so that I could sit down and be the one to figure out what he was saying when he went to commercial. It always sounded like, "Y'all dick around and mill be might back after a bird from our bonsor."

I'd sit there thinking, "Did he just say 'might back' or did Buckwheat just grow up and get a talk show?"

I saw one show where he had Howard Stern on as his only guest. Howard Stern prides himself on being a jerk. Then, he talks about how flat his ass is, how big his nose is, and how tiny his dick is. So, he doesn't leave you room for retaliation. He was very disrespectful to Magic. He asked Magic if he had fun contracting HIV, and Magic just being a nice man sat there and tried to smile it off. If that was me, I would've spit in his mouth right in the middle of that question and I wouldn't have stopped there. I would've leaned over and bit him and drew blood and then asked him, "Now, did you have bun catching HIB? Y'all dick around we'll be might back after a word from our bonsor."

After that show, Magic should have fired everybody that worked with him. He was ill advised. I knew Magic's show was in trouble from the start. His first show Magic picked Arnold Schwarzenegger as the lead guest—another man who can't talk! I didn't understand either one of them during the interview.

Magic: Oh, Arnold, you beally great man. I dor yo lass moobie. It was babulous. The way they blow you up, man, that was fantastic. I fell like I was watching Michael Chordan duckin' fro the free trow line.
Arnold: Oh yeah, Magic. OH AHH EHH OH OOH SEE.
Magic: Juss hole on, Ahnol. We want you to binish your dory. But we wanna pay a bill right naw. Y'all dick around we'll be might back with Daffy Duck, Porky Pig, and Mike Tyson after a bird from our bonsor.

Magic and HIV

Before he had his own talk show and even after his first return to the NBA, there were always rumors that Magic Johnson was going to come out of retirement and play for the Lakers again. Now, I didn't know much about HIV, but it sure seems to make you real indecisive. Magic just could not make up his mind. He didn't know what to do with himself. Still, when he returned, I was glad to see the players embrace him. I thought there would have been a lot of controversy. I mean, there he is, coming down the court, all sweaty. You just can't play the same defense that you used to play on him.

Player: Whoops, couldn't block that one. Magic just went by me, man. Hey, coach, that's Magic! I can't check Magic.

I wouldn't be surprised if someone put on one of those outbreak costumes while defending him.

Player: You know what you got. Let's play the game!

The only player in the NBA that showed him no mercy was Dennis Rodman. He just did not care. Hell, he played him like he was HIV-positive, too. He was not afraid of the contact. He just kept throwing Magic to the ground, saying, "Look, I fucked Madonna." He didn't know what he had.

I make jokes about Magic, but the truth is I have nothing but respect for this brother, and I mean that from the heart. I cried when Magic Johnson made the announcement that he is HIV-positive. I just wasn't ready for it. Why couldn't it be Little Richard that made this announcement? I would have seen that one coming. At his press conference he would've said, "Guess what? I'm HIV-positive! HEE HEE HEE! Shut up! I started AIDS. It wasn't no green monkey. The monkey stole it from me. I had it first. I was HIV-positive when Rock Hudson was just a pebble. Shut up! I gave everybody some of this tutti-frutti, good booty."

But, no, it was Magic. Just the fact that he came forward and announced that he was HIVpositive makes him a better man than me. He risked his family, his career, and his lifestyle to tell a whole bunch of paranoid people about having the virus. There are not a lot of men that would do this. Myself included. No, you would not have got that kind of honesty from me. I would have been the skinniest brother in the NBA. Manute Bol would have been saying, "Look at how skinny this motherfucker here is. He's trying to take all of the flies!"

I would have lied my ass off at interviews.

Interviewer: Damon, rumor has it that you are sick.
Me: Man, that's bullshit. Yeah, I might have dropped a few pounds. But, you know, I'm working on my inside game. Why a brother gotta be sick?

I know what Magic was trying to do. He went public to reach out to all of those women he slept with. Of course, I would have felt that I had the same obligation because that's some foul shit to pass on to somebody. But the way I look at it, you can't take it back. So why go public? I would have made a bunch of anonymous calls or something. Get that ten-cents-a-minute calling plan. I would have been dialing my ass off.

Ring, ring, ring. "Hello. Hi, I'm sick, you're sick, too." *Click.*

Ring, ring, ring. "Hello. Hey, if you're losing weight it's not Jenny Craig." *Click.*

Ring, ring, ring. "Hello. Hey, you feel indecisive? You don't know? You got it." *Click.*

It's strange to hear guys in denial about how Magic got it. I've heard guys saying, "Man, he was kissing on Isiah Thomas that's how he got that shit."

Isiah isn't gay. And neither is Magic. The man is too tall to be gay. The brother is six-foot-nine! You'd have to climb a ladder to get into his ass.

Potential Gay Lover: Okay, Magic, we're going to try something different now. You just stand there and let me get this ladder set up. I never done it like this before. Okay, here I come . . . Shit, I still don't reach! Listen, I'll be back. I'm going to get my stilts.

Would You Rather Have HIV or O.J.?

There's something worse than having HIV, and that's O.J. I feel sorry for O.J. Simpson, I truly do. Imagine being alienated from the world, totally alone, with no one wanting to have anything to do with you. I'd take the Ebola virus over what he got. The case will always fascinate me for the effect it had on everyone, black and white. I still don't believe he did it. My blackness won't allow me to accept it, much in the same way white people believe that Elvis is still alive. Maybe I'm in denial, but I just am not going to buy it.

Of the many things in the case I can't understand, maybe the most puzzling is how he could kill two people at one time. I mean, the girl got stabbed thirty-seven times. That means that Ron Goldman didn't have to die that night because while O.J. was working on her, he should have been running. That's what I would have done. Curiosity will make you hang around for the first couple of stabs. You'll be standing there in shock, thinking, "Man, this nigger is going off." Then your feet take over and say, "Look, we're getting the fuck out of here! You see how many times he stabbed her? You wanna be next? Run!"

I don't know what happened that night. Maybe if I was there they'd have found me dead, too. But I can guarantee you two things: one, they would have found my body about eight blocks away, and two, most of those stab wounds would have been in my ass, the only thing the killer could reach while I was running. They would have found me with a knife lodged in my butt. I bet nobody would have messed with that evidence.

The funniest thing about the O.J. trial, to me, was the verdict. To see white people lose their cool was damn funny. White folks are known to maintain their composure. They don't get all emotional. You see them on the news and they calmly say, "America is at war." Or, "There's a ninety-trillion-dollar deficit." Or, "Last night, fifty-three people died in a fire." Each time with no emotion. And white people watching this would at most shake their heads and say, "Tsk, tsk."

But when O.J. was acquitted, white people lost their minds: "This is BULLSHIT! I am OUTRAGED! This is HORRIFIC! I'm FLABBERGASTED!" They were making up new words: "This is some FRAGA-NOCAL BULLSHIT!"

I thought white people were gonna riot. I was thinking, "Yeah, finally we're gonna get something out of the deal." I was up in Beverly Hills with a stack of bricks, trying to instigate a riot. "Hey, white man, you heard about the verdict? Ain't that some fraga-nocal bullshit? Here, take one of these bricks and break this Gucci window. Let's get us some!"

I didn't understand why they put him through

civil court. How do you go from criminal court to civil court? What kind of new nigger rule is that? I'm telling you, they were going to try him in every court in America. They were determined to get that brother. If they hadn't won in civil court, they'd a brought him to the People's Court, and after that the Tennis Court. "You lose this match, Mr. Simpson, and you will be found guilty."

As much as I believe that O.J. did not commit the murder, I also believe he is not a smart man. He should have taken the verdict and left the country. He should have stepped out of the courthouse and onto a plane, gone to Ireland, and become the King of the White Women. But no, he had to go put out a tape, his version of the circumstances surrounding the murder and the night in question. He started the tape off trying to discredit his wife. Not an intelligent move, considering she's dead and can't defend herself. I got some of the transcript from the video right here:

O.J. Simpson: First of all it is ludicrisp . . . uh, not to be confused with Super Sugar Crisp, to think that I would want to kill Nicole. That was just some old ass to me. You know, I tapped it a few times, dropped a few calves, then I was moving on to some bigger, better, whiter women. I mean, everybody I know slept with Nicole Brown. Marcus Allen, Byron Allen, Woody Allen, Ethan Allen, Debbie Allen. Basically all your name had to be was Allen.

Now I want to walk you all through this "stuppossed"

crime scene. The district attorney said I "stuppossedly" jumped over a wall on the night in question. Now if you know me from football or maybe one of my Hertz commercials where I jump over the car, or as of lately the high-impact aerobic workout tape, you would know I got bad knees. Ashy bad knees. There is no way I could have jumped over the wall. And I'm gonna demonstrate to you that there's no way I could've gotten over this wall by running and trying to jump ov— Oh damn! My knee! See, there's no way I can jump over this wall.

So that's half of Miss Marcia's case right out the window. Now here's the kicker. They say I "rellegedly" dropped a glove at the scene of the crime. Let me say this: I played football for some twenty-nine years. Never once did I drop the ball. So, how the fuck am I gonna drop a glove at the scene of the crime? Look at my hands. They are finely trained machines, and they can hold on to anything under any circumstances. And do you see how big they are? I can wipe my ass and scratch my head at the same time with these hands. A glove is not gonna just slip off a hand this big.

Now, I'm gonna demonstrate to you that there's no way that I could have dropped a glove at the scene of the crime because my hands are so good. Now I want you take this ball and I want you throw it. Throw it anywhere you want and I'll catch it. I don't care where you throw it. . . . You know what, throw it over the wall. Go ahead, I'll show you there's no way I could've dropped it. Here I go, I'm running as fast as I can! I'm jumping over the wall and . . . I've got it! Heh, heh, heh. Still got the skills! Let me jump back over the wall. There, you see, there's no way I would have dropped the glove at the scene of the crime.

O.J. has custody of his kids, which is nice. I'd sure love to be there for playtime because you know the kids are scared of him.

O.J.'d be wandering around the house, checking under tables and furniture, saying, "Y'all come on out now! Daddy's not gonna hurt you. Where y'all at? And where are all of the knives in this house?"

I heard O.J. say in an interview that white people still love him. Is he crazy? White people are scared of him. The white half of his children is afraid of him. What's he talking about, when he says, "The white people I know are very supportive of me. Wherever I go they're standing outside, lighting candles, holding up signs with my name on them. They actually give me the thumbs-up sign whenever they see me."

He can't really be this stupid. First, it's not the thumbs-up sign the white people are giving you, they're actually aiming at your ass. Second, they're lighting candles because they can't light a cross. They're praying that one of those candles falls and catches his black ass on fire and burns him to death. And third, O.J., you need to read the signs because they say KILL THE NIGGER.

White People Loving Me

After I started on *In Living Color*, I had a problem O.J. is probably never going to have again: white people showing their love toward me. Sometimes things really got intense.

White Fan: Hey, you're Damon Wayans, from *In Living Color*, right?

Me: Ah, yeah, how are you?

White Fan: Gee whiz, I can't believe it's you. Man, I love you.

Me: Thank you very much.

White Fan: No, you don't understand, dude, I really love you, you're the tits, man. I mean, my whole family loves you. This is my eighteen-year-old daughter—she loves you, too. Why don't you take a picture with her!

Me: Sure.

White Fan: No, get closer. Hug her, man, it's okay. She loves you. Go ahead kiss her. Give her some tongue, dude. Don't be shy, we love you. Ah, what the hell, go on, fuck her, man, you deserve it. You're special. You're not like the other black guys. Hey, where are you going, Damon? We love you!

This really messed with my mind. If you hear white folks say, "You're not like the other black guys, you're special," over and over again, you can really start to believe it. Until the cops pull you over.

Police Officer: All right, nigger, license and registration.

Me: But officer, I'm Damon Wayans—I'm not like the others, I'm special.

Police Officer: So is my .38. Now, put your hands where I can see them before I put a special bullet in your special ass.

Being Famous Ain't Fun

Sometimes people ask me what the hardest thing about being me is. And I answer, "Being famous all day long."

This is what people think my day is like:

I wake up with three beautiful women in bed with me, then, I go to my window in my velvet robe, with a glass of Dom P., wave to my fans, then the Gucci truck shows up with something to wear then I go to the bank, count bags of money, come back home in my chauffeur-driven Rolls, while being fed grapes by three different girls in the backseat. Say hello to my wife, give her money, give my kids money, play with my lion, have an orgy, fall asleep to Barry White and Whitney Houston singing live in my living room on my piano, wake up and do it all over again.

Well, it's nothing like that, except giving my wife money. Sometimes you don't feel like being famous. Like, when you've got a toothache, or you're being audited, or a relative dies. You just want to be by your damn self. I remember one time while I was in New York and I had this really bad stomach virus. I was throwing up and had a really bad case of diarrhea. I walked over to the drugstore to get something to calm my stomach. I went to the counter to pay for it:

Cashier: Hey, you're Damon Wayans, right?

Me: Yes. How much is this Kaopectate? I gotta hurry up and get out of here.

Cashier: Hold on, buddy. You gotta give me your autograph before you leave.

Me: Look, man, I'm really not feeling well.

Cashier: Aw, come on. Don't be such a "Homey the Clown." Hey, Billy, Damon Wayans from *In Living Color* is here.

Now Billy came over.

Billy: Hey, Damon, I really love your work. Gimme two snaps up.

Me: I'm about to give you more than two snaps.

Billy: Come on, dude. Do one of your characters for us.

Me: Okay, I'll do Anton the Bum.

Billy: Jesus Christ, what's that smell?

Me: My pickle jar must be backed up. HA HA HA.

Finally, I left the store.

Billy: Dude, he must be a method actor because I really believed he had diarrhea. He smelled like shit, dude!

Mike and the Hit Man

On *In Living Color*, we used to get people upset. But we were just having fun and you can't take comedy serious. Mike Tyson got really upset once. That's one brotha I didn't want to make mad. Keenen was the one that did the impression of Mike in a sketch called "Three Champs and a Baby." Mike thought it was me.

One day, I walked out of a jewelry store where I was looking for a gift for my wife. Tommy Hearns and Mike were standing on the sidewalk.

Mike shouted, "Dhere he is!"

I tried to run back inside, but the store had one of those electronic doors that lock on your black ass. I was nervous as hell. Mike grabbed me and bit me on my neck.

"I saw you doing me on TV," Mike said, his veins popping on his head. "I didn't like that, funnyman. You think you're funny, don't you?"

"No, Mike, that wasn't me. It was my bro—"

"Don't try to lie to me," Mike's voice went up a notch. "Tommy saw you, too. Tommy, didn't you see him doing me on TV?"

"That's wite," Tommy mumbled. "I was with the

nother side, she said go on with the nother side and go on with the nother side."

"What did he just say?" I asked, as politely as I could.

"He said yes," Mike answered. "I don't want to see you doing me on TV anymore, funnyman. If I do, I'm gonna design a punch dat will make your wiver bleed."

"Yes, sir, Mr. Tyson." Man, I was lucky to get out of that alive.

Now don't go thinking I'm a punk. I mean normally if another cat grabs me, even if I think he can beat me, I'm going to fake it. Put some bass in my voice and say, "Yeah, you better hold me, motherfucker! Hold me tight, jack, 'cause if you let me go you're dead!"

There was none of that with Mike. I just laid there like a bitch in his arms. What am I gonna do against Iron Mike Tyson? If Mike came up to me and said, "Listen. I want to fuck you in the ass." The toughest thing that I could say back would be, "For how long? See, 'cause I need some sort of time frame, my brother. You just not gonna be fucking me in my ass all day long. Now, you got about three hours to do what you got to do then the ass reverts back to me."

A Bodyguard's Bitch

I was in New York a couple of months ago putting the final touches on a film. The production company hired a bodyguard for me. I didn't like it. To tell the truth, it kind of made me feel uncomfortable. I had this big guy opening doors for me, pulling out chairs, pushing people out of the way. I felt like I was this guy's bitch. One time I think I heard him say, "Back up, everyone, Miss Wayans is coming through!"

That's one reason why I don't have security. Another reason is, I don't think that I'm famous enough to have a bodyguard. You ever see somebody who shouldn't have a bodyguard with a bodyguard? That's the funny thing about LA. You'll see a big crowd, a lot of commotion, and you run over to see what's going on. You push your way to the front of the crowd. When you finally get there you see ... Scott Baio?!

The final reason is I figure God is my bodyguard and he gives me the good sense to know where to be and where not to be. There's always a sign to let you know if trouble is around. If I go out to a party and a guy is standing in front of the club saying something like, "If y'all don't let me in, I'm gonna shoot everybody up in this motherfucka!" See, that's the sign. I'm not hanging around to see if he was bullshittin'. I don't want to see what kind of gun he has, whether or not the police are gonna show up in time, or who it was that pissed that brother off. I'm taking my ass home to watch a video. It's a Blockbuster night. You can't get shot watching porno. You may shoot, but you won't get shot.

You Don't Remember My Movies, Do You?

I'm doing standup again because my movie career wasn't happening. I wasn't happy with it. I had turned into a total whore, doing movies that I didn't care about. I just did them for the money. I felt like that little cartoon penguin—Chilly Willy. I was just being greedy. They would say:

Hollywood: You want to make a movie about basketball?
Me: Mmhmm. That's nice.
Hollywood: How about boxing? Do you know how to box?
Me: Yes, I box. I'll hit-em like this and hit-em like that.

But even at my lowest, there was one line I wouldn't cross.

Hollywood: Would you play a slave?
Me: No! I'll get the hell out before I sell out!

Amistad

A lot of people ask me if I've ever thought about doing a dramatic role. The answer is yes. I tried to get a role in the movie *Amistad*, which was directed by Steven Spielberg. Unfortunately, Steven wouldn't even see me. They said I wasn't black enough. I was a little offended by that at first. But then I thought about the audition process and what I would've been subjected to, and I started to feel a little better. After all, it's hard to get your dignity back after auditioning for a slave role.

Spielberg: Action!

Me: I is da bestest nigger you gots, sa. I's can picks da cotton with my feets if I has ta. I's do anything to be yo slave, sa. You can beat me and I don't bleed much. Plus, I's tells on all the other niggas. Please, please, massa, don't give me my freedom.

Spielberg: Cut!

Me: Thank you, Mr. Spielberg, for giving me the opportunity to showcase my talents.

Spielberg: You're welcome. But I'm sorry, Damon, you're just not nigger enough. I'm looking for someone more coonish. I need a more . . . Danny Gloverish type.

Adopt a Nigger

When I found out that Spielberg has two black kids, I was amazed. What I want to know is, where the hell did he get these black kids from? Are they a prop left over from *The Color Purple*? Probably after the movie he was walking around the set, saying "Okay, I want those two spears, Oprah's handkerchief, Harpo's hat, and wrap those two little niggers up over there."

I guess when you have a lot of money you can do anything. I hope one day to adopt me a little white kid. Maybe a nice little Jewish boy. He'll be able to help me out with my taxes and manage my career. We need a lawyer in the family. I'm tired of all these damned comedians.

A Cool Slave

Even if Spielberg didn't want to consider me for *Amistad*, it seems every time I look up there's some Hollywood producer coming to me with a slave role. I can't play a slave. I refuse to play one 'cause I've got four kids. How are my kids ever going to respect me if they see me being beaten and treated like a slave?

Me: Little Damon, get off that chair before I spank your behind!
Son: Yeah, you weren't so tough when the massa was kickin' your ass.

Besides that, there has never been a cool slave role. Every time you see a brother playing a slave he's always whining and crying. If I had to play a slave, I'd want to play the one that gets raped by the white woman, and has to go to trial and defend himself:

Slave: I didn't wants to do it, yo honor. She forceded herself on me. I was outs in da fields bustin' up the chifferobe. I don't even know what the chifferobe is. But they say I have to bust it up. So, I bust it up.

Then, I hears Missy, off in the distance. She comes just a jumping and a skipping singing "Yankee Doodle Dandy." And I's knows somethin' was a wrong, Massa, so when she comes close to me I looks away. She said "Timbuck, look at me." I said, "No, Missy, yo whiteness is hurtin' my eyes." Then she comes over and toucheded me on my privacy. My eyes sprung up as wide as dey can be. I said, "Missy, you don't want to let this here monkey out of the bag. 'Cause you know once you go black you don't come back."

Missy said, "Timbuck, I wants to give you head." Shucks, I thought she was gonna put me in charge of the other negroes. I want's to get ahead, sa. But she had her lil' mind on somethin' else. She gets to kissin' me all over my black face with them little thin lips of hers. It felt like two pieces of baloney on the side of my face. Then, she says, "Timbuck, I loves you." And she put her head down there where no white women's head belongs, sa. . . . That's right. In the jungle. Then, she looked up at me and there was this shadow going across her face. Must have been one of them trees or somethin'. And I remember she look up at me and said, "Timbuck, yous might hang for this." I said, "Yassum, but you gonna choke first, Missy."

Tattoo and Corky

When I get bitter about my acting career, I just think about the other people that had it worse than I do. Guys like Hervé Villechaize, the little guy that played Tattoo on *Fantasy Island*. Imagine how tough it was for him. I mean, what possessed him to look into the mirror and say, "I'm going to be an actor. I want be the next Latin lover."

What people don't know is, Hervé didn't get discovered. He had to audition like every other actor in Hollywood. I'm sure there were several parts he auditioned for that he didn't get because he was just totally wrong for the role. As an actor you are taught to believe that you can play anything. So, Hervé would walk into the casting office confident.

Hervé: Hello, my name is Hervé Villechaize and I am here to audition for the part of Superman.

Casting Director: Well, you may not be right for the part.

Hervé: What do you mean I'm wrong for the part? I got a big chest. I got little legs but my chest is wide. You can stand me on a table or something. Just let me play the part. Please give me a chance. I drove all the way here on my Big Wheel so I could read for the part. Look up in the sky. It's a bird. It's da plane, da plane, da plane!

Casting Director: Well, thank you very much for coming in. That was great. Don't call us, we'll call you.
Hervé: Aw, fuck you. You don't know talent when you see it.

The next day he'd be back in the casting office for something else he wasn't right for.

Hervé: Hi, my name is Hervé Villechaize. I want to audition for the part of the Terminator.
Casting Director: Sorry, but we just gave the role to Arnold Schwarzenegger.
Hervé: Aw, fuck you! You don't know talent when you see it. I'll be back.
Casting Director: Hey, that's a great line. We should put it in the movie. I'll be right back.

The worst thing that can happen to an actor is for the public to know him for a single role. An actor does all of this work over the span of a career and all the public can remember is the one thing. For example, Jimmie Walker is forty-nine years old, has a big gut, and looks like a swollen rat. People see him and all they can think to say is "Dy-no-mite." Jimmie doesn't want to hear that shit. The same thing happened to Hervé. He will forever be remembered as Tattoo, the guy who said "da plane, da plane." When he was out in public, it must've been a nightmare.

Brother: Yo, man, that's the dude. That's the little mother-fucka from that show, *Fantasy Island*! Yo, little man, say that shit that you be sayin' about the plane. Yo, me and my boys be laughin' off at that.

Tattoo: Please, I'm standing in line here to get some hemorrhoid cream. Please don't bother me right now.

Brother on the Street: Come on, shorty, just say it. Just once, man.

Tattoo: Okay, okay. You want me to say it even with hemorrhoids? Here you go. Look, boss, da plane, da plane, da plane. You satisfied now?

Brother on the Street: Yo, fuck you. You ain't that good anyway. Big-headed freak!

I believe that's one of the reasons Hervé killed himself. I heard that before his death, he would hang out in bars getting drunk with his best friend Chris Burke, Corky from *Life Goes On*.

Hervé: No one loves Hervé. They only like Tattoo. Tattoo this, Tattoo that. They can kiss Tattoo's ass!

Chris: I know what you mean, Hervé. 'Cause no one cares about me either. It's all about Corky.

Hervé: You know something, Corky, I never liked Mr. Roarke from *Fantasy Island*. He was an asshole, a real son of a bitch. You know that in the five years that we worked together, he never once shook my hand?

Chris: Why not?

Hervé: He said to touch my little fingers gave him the willies. He said it would make his palms itch for the rest of the day, if I ever shook his hand. That son of a bitch! He makes me sick to my stomach.

Chris: Well, life goes on.

Hervé: I guess you're right, but he didn't have to treat me with disrespect. I'm a man, not a little boy. Do you know that he was the one that made me call him boss? I said to him, "But why do I have to call you boss?" And he said, "Because you're down by my balls." And then, he used me to make the girls laugh. Always trying to impress the *Fantasy Island* girls. His big joke was every time we'd do a scene together he'd find a reason to put his ass in my face. One time we were filming a two-hour special and he ate six burritos with extra guacamole and a jalapeno sauce. He didn't have to do that. Well, I'll tell you this, the girls wouldn't think he was so sexy if they knew what Ricardo Montalban's ass smells like!

Chris: Well, life goes on. I mean, I could think of one hundred reasons to be upset. I'm not bitter. So what, I didn't get the part in *Rainman*. Who cares, they went with somebody else for *My Left Foot*? Even though I would've been perfect for *Sling Blade*, I'm not going to wallow in self-pity. You know what? We have to count our blessings. It could always be worse.

Hervé: You got that right. I mean, we could be niggers, right?

Chris: I'll drink to that!

Gary Coleman

Hervé's not the only short guy who's had problems. I heard the other day that they arrested Gary Coleman. Damn, what's the world coming to when little Gary Coleman starts getting arrested? What's sad is he's been reduced to working as a security guard in a shopping mall. I don't know what he's guarding at four feet tall—must be somebody's nuts or something.

"What you talking bout, mister?" He'll be screaming, "Can't touch these nuts, brother!"

Gary got back in the spotlight when he had an argument with a woman at the mall. Apparently, the woman wanted an autograph. He said, "Not while I'm on duty." So, she got mad and called him a little has-been. And then he punched her in the thigh. I feel sorry for him. He started out so little and cute. People were coming up to him saying, "Awww, look how sweet." Then, he stayed four feet tall and grew a beard, and started scaring people. "Oh shit, what is that thing?"

"What you talkin' 'bout, mister?" Gary would say, his lower lip sticking out.

"Oh God, it talks! It's a little black Ewok! Run!"

Oprah's Looking Good

I saw Oprah recently on the cover of *Vogue* magazine. Damn, she looks good! Nothing like *The Color Purple* days. The woman lost over fifty pounds, which is an amazing feat. But she had to lose weight because there was a time when Oprah would come down the aisle on her show and knock people off their chairs with her big ass. I remember one show in particular that was really frightening:

Oprah: Okay, we have a caller. Who's on the line?
Caller: Hello, Oprah, my name is Harry and I'm calling from inside your ass.
Oprah: Really?
Caller: Yeah, you remember last week when you dropped the microphone? Well, I was right behind you when you bent over to pick it up.
Oprah: What is your point, caller?
Caller: Well, I just wanted to say, I like what you did with your ass. It's really comfortable in here and I don't think I ever want to come out. They're actually building a mall on the right cheek of your ass.
Oprah: Thank you, caller. If you see Stedman tell him I don't care how long he hides out in there, I'm still not going to promote his book.

Ain't that a bitch. Stedman Graham wrote a book titled, *How to Be Successful in Business*. It should have been one page. Chapter One: "Marry Oprah." He's a lucky man, because if I were Oprah—smart, rich, with my own successful talk show—not only would I have stayed fat, but I would've gotten fatter. I would've made it my goal to gain a pound a day. I would have made him lay down with me and feed me cake and ice cream and tell me how pretty I am and how much he loved me for who I am. That would've been his job. Then he would've added a second chapter to his book. Chapter Two: "How to Kill Your Woman and Hide Her Fat Body Without Getting Caught."

Dr. Death

Stedman could have gone to Dr. Kevorkian for advice on how to get away with killing someone. I'm glad they finally convicted this madman for murder. I mean, what kind of profession is that, where you kill people and call yourself a doctor? He must have been the worst student in his class. His professor must have said to him, "Maybe you should try law. You're really not good at keeping these people alive."

Kevorkian answered, "Hmmmm, maybe I'll be a death doctor. Carve my own niche."

Do you know this man has killed over a hundred people? That's too much power for any man to possess. And he tries to justify it by saying he's helping them make a transition to a better place. Do you know how many black men are down in county jail right now trying to use that same excuse?

They're standing before the judge, saying, "Your honor, I was trying to help these people get to the other side. And I knew they wouldn't be able to get there with all that money they had. So I simply took their lives and wallets. But they are in a better place now. They don't need all these material things that this world says you're supposed to have."

I'm sure that in the beginning they were mercy killings and Kevorkian was sincerely trying to help these people by easing their suffering. But, like any job, after you do it over and over again, you start getting bored. You start looking for new ways to keep yourself entertained. Over time, he started toying with the way he took them out.

Kevorkian: All right, Mr. Nadlehaff, just sign right here. And then I can help you make that transition. Now, why don't we do something a little different here? We'll put a little acid in your IV, just to mix it up a little. Help speed up the transition a little.

By the twenty-fifth guy, he tried something even more creative. He walked in the room with a mallot behind his back.

Kevorkian: How you feeling there, Mr. Johnson?
Mr. Johnson: Not too good.
Kevorkian: Great. Listen, I was talking to the nurse. And . . . hey, is that your wife over there?
Mr. Johnson: Where?
Crack!
Kevorkian: Another one bites the dust. Yeah!

I guess by the time he got to the seventy-fifth guy, he just walked into the room with a loaded gun.

Kevorkian: All right, fucker. You've got three seconds to run.
Smith: Aaahhhh!!

Recently, he's been feeling a little feisty and that's what got him caught. He got way too creative and filmed it.

Kevorkian: Hello there, Mary. How are you doing, sweetheart?
Mary: Not good.
Kevorkian: Great. Listen, Mare, do you trust me?
Mary: Yes, doctor.
Kevorkian: Good. 'Cause I've designed a trip to the other side that's gonna make you the envy of the deceased. This will be my greatest transition of them all. Okay, I want you to take your thumb and put it in your ass.
Mary: Like this?
Kevorkian: Yes, that's right. Now I want you to grab hold of this electric cord. Okay, wave good-bye.
BZZZZZZTTTT!

How Fat Can You Get?

I was looking through some old *Jet* magazines the other day and I came across the name Walter Hudson. Remember him? He was that fat guy who was confined to his bed because he weighed sixteen hundred pounds. Now, this just doesn't make any sense to me. At some point he must have looked down and said, "Damn, I can't find my penis. Maybe I need to work out a little."

But no, Walter refused to acknowledge the signs. He just laid there and continued to eat. I blame his family because they were the ones that kept feeding him. At some point if you love someone you don't encourage that kind of behavior. For breakfast Walter would have two pounds of bacon, one dozen eggs, a large loaf of bread, and then he'd wash it down with a gallon of orange juice. You're not supposed to give him all that food. The family should have hidden a few of the eggs, or maybe switched to turkey bacon. It ain't like he's going to get mad. And even if he does, what is he going to do, get up and kick your ass? I think somebody in his family was making money off of him. They had some little sideshow. The billboard read:

STEP RIGHT UP. SEE THE AMAZING WALTER HUDSON EAT
A DOZEN EGGS IN ONE MINUTE FLAT. ONLY TWENTY DOLLARS!
FOR AN EXTRA FIVE DOLLARS WALTER WILL ALSO EAT TWO
POUNDS OF UNCOOKED BACON!
*Satisfaction guaranteed or your money back.

This man was so big he had to call the fire department to help him go to the bathroom. I guess twenty minutes after he ate that big breakfast he'd pick up the phone. "Hello? It's on."

The fire truck would arrive with sirens going and people from all over the neighborhood would show up in front of the house. The squad of fireman would haul his huge body down the hall and into the bathroom, then, with their gas masks on, they use the jaws of life to hold his ass open long enough for him to do his business. The neighbors would let out a cheer until that smell hit them. Then, they'd have to call the sanitation department to clean the mess up.

Got to Leave LA

Los Angeles has nice weather most of the year and if you're going to work in show business, this is where you've got to live. But I've got to get out of LA for one very important reason: earthquakes. We had one a couple of years ago that scared the life out of me. I haven't shit on myself since I was about five, but the day of that earthquake I let a chunk go. I was especially afraid because I have children to think about. I remember I was standing in front of my house butt naked, thinking, "Man, I hope them kids make it out here. And I hope they're smart enough to wake up their mama, 'cause this place is shaking."

The funny thing is that Angelenos are not fazed by earthquakes. After almost every earthquake they'll be saying, "Dude, that wasn't the big one."

I guess they're waiting for the whole state to break off and fall in the ocean. See, I'm packing 'cause I know that the ground is saying, "Get the fuck up off me!"

I did some research and found out that the largest earthquake ever recorded took place in Anchorage, Alaska. It was a 9.2 on the Richter scale. See that's twenty-two percent stronger than the

Northridge earthquake we had in 1994. It shook for over fifteen minutes. So that little 6.5 we had was a gay earthquake compared to a 9.2. This thing's like, "Rumble, rumble, rumble . . . knock this over, knock that over. Ooh, I'm exhausted. I'm out of here."

I saw footage of the Anchorage earthquake. It was terrifying. I wonder what goes through your mind during fifteen minutes of earthquake? I guess the first thirty seconds you're thinking, "Oh my God, I'm gonna die." Then twenty seconds later you're thinking, "Damn, when is this shit gonna stop?" Five minutes into the earthquake you just say, "Fuck it, I might as well go to work. This must be the norm. Let me go brush my teeth. Man, I ain't scrubbed so well before! Scramble myself some eggs and get a quickie in with my wife. Baby, I may not be this active again until the next big earthquake. Hang on!"

The Pimp and the President

Let me tell you, being in show business, I really get to meet the sickos of the world. And it seems like everybody wants to be in show business. Everybody! I met a pimp from East St. Louis on my last movie who was trying to break into show business. He was on the set doing extra work with two of the ugliest hoes I've ever seen. He walked up to me one day and pitched a movie to me.

"Hey, Damonson—how can I get some dialogue up in this motherfucker? Man, they got me doing this extra work. I'm too pretty for this shit, nigger. It makes me look bad in front of my bitches. But listen, I got this movie for you. I got this script I wrote. . . . What you laughing at, nigger? I seen *Blankman*, you better listen! No, nigger, that movie was not funny. My retarded son didn't even laugh at that movie, and that boy laughs at car accidents.

"Now, look, I got this movie about these alien bitches that come from another planet and they got three titties. Two up top and one right above the navel. And everyone is trying to freak with these alien bitches but what they don't know is that that third tittie is poisonous. It got poison tittie juice that kills you in three days. And everybody's dying all around the world.

Over in Russia they're dying. Over in China their little dicks are falling off. Looks like somebody spilled a bag of rice over there. So the president of the United States sleeps with one of these alien bitches and he's only got seventy-two hours to live. So he calls a meeting at the White House.

"'What to do? What to do?'" the president asks.

"Then Colin Powell stands up and says, 'We need a pimp up in this motherfucker.'

"So the president says, 'Yeah, that's a good idea. Don't you have one in your family?'

"Anyway, they go out to Washington, D.C., and find the baddest pimp they can find. His name is Silky Smooth. That's who you gonna play, Damonson. Silky struts up in the White House stairs. He got on a lime green jumpsuit with bright orange shoes and a big leopard skin hat. Just like the shit I got on right now. He walk up to the president and says, 'What's the deal motherfucker, I'm losing money being here. What you want with me?'

"The president says, 'Mr. Silky, please sit down. May I get you something to drink?'

"Silky says, 'I don't want nothing to drink, this is the White House. Bring me some cocaine.' So they go out and get the best cocaine they can find. They get him some shit out of Marion Barry's personal stash. While Silky's sitting there, getting his freeze on he says, 'I'm gonna help you out, Mr. President, 'cause I know you like niggers. But, I'm gonna want something in return.'

"The president says, 'Anything, Silky. We'll make every Tuesday Big Hat Day just for you.'

"Silky says, 'I don't want that shit. I want your daughter in my stable.'

"Well, the President's wife jumps up and says, 'Oh no, you ain't taking my baby, no no no.'

"And Silky walks over and slaps the shit out of her. *BAM!* He uses one of your lines, Damonson: 'Silky don't play that shit.' He picked her up and said, 'I'm taking you, too. You're my first lady now. Get your ass up and go get that little bitch and wait in the car for me.'

"The president comes over and says, 'Silky, thank goodness you took them. Between Whitewater and my ugly daughter I almost didn't get reelected!'

"So now Silky got to find the antidote to save the President. He goes out and has to talk to them alien bitches to find out where their leader's at. He walks up to them and he says, 'Hey, ho, who's your pimp?' The aliens don't speak no English, though. They start speaking all of that gibberish. See Silky knows they don't speak English but everybody understands an ass whupping. So Silky gets to kicking them bitches' asses pimp style. *POW, POW, POW!* He takes his hanger out and heats that shit up with a lighter. *WHAM, WHAM, WHAM!* Them bitches started speaking English better than Margaret Thatcher.

"She says, 'Bob Dole is my pimp daddy.'

"So here's the surprise, Damonson. You find out that Bob Dole is really Bob Dolomite, a pimp from another planet called Tittoris. He failed at becoming the president of the United States, but that's not going to stop him from pimping the world! You find out that this motherfucker didn't get his arm blown up in the war. He slammed it in his spaceship door!

"Silky goes to his house in the middle of the night to get the antidote for the poison titty juice. He unlocks the door with his hanger and tiptoes in. He looks around and sees Bob Dolomite sleeping, but he don't got his arm on. Bob Dolomite takes the shit off at night and puts it in a glass case like that motherfucker from that movie *Enter the Dragon.* Silky sees the arm in the case on the dresser with the antidote laying inside the hand.

"When he tries to remove the antidote, Bob Dolomite jumps out of the bed and says, 'Hey, nigger, put my arm down!'

"And then Bob Dolomite starts twisting his leg around. See, this motherfucker comes apart like Mr. Potatohead. He twists his whole leg off and uses it as a weapon. *WHAM, WHAM, WHAM!* Silky goes down. Bob Dolomite hops over to him and is about to drop the nub on his head to finish him off. Silky sees him coming and kicks his other leg out and it breaks off. Now Bob Dolomite starts crawling toward him like the Terminator.

"Silky grabs the antidote and starts running for the window. Bob Dolomite twists his dick off and it turns into dynamite. He then bites off the tip and throws it at Silky. Silky sees the dynamite coming and he kicks it back and it goes up Bob Dolomite's ass and he explodes. So, what do you think?"

Actually, it did sound better than *Blankman.*

Mr. Bill

I don't know what the big deal is with the president getting a little head. I think the president needs some every now and then to help relax him. Imagine what it's like running a country. A little head would take the edge off and make him more generous in his decision making.

President: Ahhh, ohhh yeah! What a great idea, let's put a little more money in welfare reform. That's it for today, I need a nap. *Zzzzzzzz.*

I have a problem with the face that gave the head. Come on Bill, Monica Lewinsky? You could do better than that. Kennedy had Marilyn Monroe. You could have had the *Baywatch* girls, *Playboy* bunnies, Cindy Crawford, Elle Macpherson. All of them would have given the president head if they thought it was a matter of national security. But Monica? Yuck. I wouldn't trust that big fat girl around my dick. She might think it's a frank and try to eat it. Monica Lewinsky didn't need any more protein in her diet, what she needed was some fiber. Mr. Clinton should have let her toss his salad.

Mrs. Bill

Many people aren't aware that the Clintons' visit to Africa was really Hillary's idea. The president didn't really want to go, but Hillary said, "You want to fuck around, I'm fucking around, too. Now, you take me where the dick is so long that they can't wear drawers!"

So, there they were standing around all those Africans. And Bill was uncomfortable and didn't know what to say. Then he thought he could try make things right.

President: I just want to apologize for your ancestors' being taken over to our country and forced into the degradation of slavery.

African Leader: Hey, redface white man! Shut the hell up. We don't want to hear that sorry bullshit. Go apologize to the niggers in America. We are happy here. They are the ones that need your sympathy. We are here for white pussy. Now, back up, motherfucka, you are standing on my dick!

Mo' Money

I found out that one of my partners, Larry, is in jail now. He got twenty five years for something that he didn't do—he didn't run fast enough. I always knew this brother was going to jail 'cause he's one of them dudes that wanted to make it in life but he wanted to get over. He was a con artist. Always had a plan. I called him the "street business man." I saw him when he got out of jail the last time.

"What's up, D?" he said. "Yo, it's good to see you, man. I heard you was out there in California, man. You doin' comedy now, right? You funny? Go ahead—say something funny. Aw, man, you need an audience and shit. . . . Look, you keep doing it, man. You might be like the next Bugs Bunny or something. Yeah, but I ain't got time for no Three Stooges type silliness. I'm trying to get me some income coming in. Word! Yo, this what I'm gonna do. I'm gonna get me a full-time job at McDonald's, then I'm gonna work my way up to manager, and let my boys come and rob the place. Mo' money, mo' money! See, I take all that stolen money and throw it in the bank. I won't touch that. I'll just step off, ya know. Let the interest fuck with that. It will be like *boom* . . . Mo' money, mo' money.

"See, I'm gonna do this every other day. So they don't catch on, 'cause I don't want to go to McJail or nothing, you know. Word. I'd be in the cell with that Hamburglar he be bugging me out with that head and shit.

"Yo, then clock this—I'm gonna let my lady forge checks, right? 'Cause she works in the bank. Then I'm gonna let her prostitute on the side. You know, just in case the bank thing don't work out—she can have something to fall back on. Now this is only part-time, see? 'Cause I can't have no full-time ho living in my house.

"Then dig this, I'm gonna adopt me a kid. One of them foster childs. 'Cause they pay you to take their ass. And I'm gonna let him sell joints in school. Mo' money, mo' money! See, this is good for the kid, too. 'Cause it teaches him responsibility, right? 'Cause if he messes up my money, I'm gonna hurt him. Now I figure every day before he goes to school, I throw a hundred joints in his lunch box—get him one of those Fred Flintstone lunch boxes 'cause kids need that type of thing, you know. And then I send him on out the door. Go make that money, son. Now if he gets busted, I just come to school and play the father role.

"'What's up, teachers? No, tell me what happened. I don't wanna know your name, I don't want to shake your hand, I just want the facts. Fuck that. Tell me, what was my little white son doing?'

"Then I'll play all surprised. 'Oh snap, he was doing what? I am so surprised!'

"And since this is a teacher, right, I'll start throwing my big words on 'em. 'Circumcise me. Flatulate the information, 'cause the whole constipation got my scrotum detached. No, no, no, let me shed my foreskin on the issue. You retain your liquids while I masturbate my ambeonic fluids. So this whole thing is supercalafragalistic expealladocious.'

"See, when the teachers see how smart I am, they'll probably put me in charge of the PTA. Then I'll start selling crack to the parents. Mo' money, mo' money, mo' money!"

I Love Rap

I love rap music. I grew up on it. I actually wanted to be a rap artist, but my lyrics made me laugh and that's not what rap's supposed to do. It's supposed to make you want to kill. The thing that I like about rap is that every time you think it's over they take it to another level. At one point they were doing these rap love songs, which was all right. I appreciate brothers trying to express a sensitive side of themselves, but the shit . . . was rather corny:

> I was walking down the block the other day
> I saw a young lady, I didn't know what to say.
> She had lovey dovey hair, and lovey dovey eyes.
> Her lovey dovey dovey had me hypnotized.
> Then, I went to her house,
> I saw a little mouse.
> He ran over there
> Near her underwear.
> I need her job.

There are some rappers who can't do a love song. They are just too hard. Like DMX. I want to hear DMX make a rap love song. It would probably go something like this:

I know these two bitches
with hair shorter than stitches.
One is into voodoo,
and the other smells like doo-doo.
But I love them oh so,
even though they both hoes.

Fishbone

I went to see this band called Fishbone. Now I know black people are saying, "What the hell is a Fishbone? Got one caught in my throat once. Is that it or is it a soul food restaurant?"

No. Fishbone is a group of brothers that play that heavy metal music. It's that stuff that you see on MTV and turn from. When I saw the brothers had dreads in their hair, tattoos on their arms, and their nipples pierced—I knew I was in for some different shit. One of them picked up the guitar and started knocking shit over—amps, mike stands, and people. There was nothing but white folks in the crowd. They were all yelling out, "Radical, dude! Radical!"

Another one of the guys from Fishbone jumped into the audience and they caught him and passed him around like a joint. See, that can only happen with white people. You can't jump on no niggers. Black people have this understanding. If I pay thirty-five dollars for a ticket, keep your ass on stage. I won't come up there and fuck with your amps and you don't come down here and fuck with my clothes. As much as black folks love Bobby Brown, if he were to jump off the stage and into the audience, that shit would part like the Red Sea. Bobby would be lying on his back, moaning, and brothers would walk over, shaking their heads saying, "It's your prerogative."

They were also slam dancing at this concert, which is nothing like the dancing you see on *Soul Train*. I just don't understand it. The dance floor is filled with only guys, for one. I saw two white boys in particular look at each other from across the room. Both guys took a shot of their drinks, backed up, and ran full speed into each other. They collapsed on the floor, then got up and started fighting. If they were doing this to each other, imagine what they would do to my black ass if I joined in. I had to leave. But before I left, I kind of got into it a little. As I walked through the crowd, I was sneakin' some of the poor bastards—punching people in the eye, pulling hair, pinchin' titties—when I left, there were about twelve people lying on the floor. I heard someone say, "That's Damon Wayans, he's a great dancer. Look what he did to my nuts!"

Rap Attacks

I can't believe that rappers are killing each other. Over what, lyrics? How ignorant can that be? I can just see some angry rapper saying, "Hey, man, that's my shit! I rhymed 'now' with 'cow.' So, you remember that's my shit. Now and cow! Don't even think about using it!"

I hope this kind of ignorant shit doesn't start happening in the comedy world, "Man, did you hear Eddie Murphy shot Chris Rock because Rock stole his doo-doo joke? Yeah, man, Eddie shot him dead. Eddie says that he wants his doo-doo joke back."

Rappers

There's a real contradiction with rappers. They can be so poetic on their albums. Lyrics like,

> I'm innovative, extremely creative,
> I look African, but I'm an American Native.
> Like the Indian I'm brave,
> like the Jew, I'm a slave.
> My real name is Dave,
> I take dignity to my grave.

Their lyrics are just so fluid, you'd swear they were educated. But if you sit one of them down for a one-on-one interview, you feel like you're talking to a third grader.

Interviewer: So, Intelligent B, why don't you explain to us the history of rap and the hip hop genre?

Intelligent B: Well, you know it's like . . . trying to represent. Keeping it real, you know what I mean?

Interviewer: Ahh, yeah? So, Intelligent B, let me ask you a different question. Maybe you didn't understand the last one. Do you think that rap transcends culture and social status?

Intelligent B: Word.

Interviewer: Word?

Intelligent B: No doubt.

Interview: Let me try one more question. Do you think rap is a fad? Do you think it'll fade? Like bellbottoms and high-heel sneakers?

Intelligent B: Yo, it's like cigarettes, you know what I'm saying?

Interviewer: No. I don't know what the fuck you're saying. And how the hell did you get a name like 'Intelligent'? Why don't you just rap your damn answers to me?

Part 2

Marriage & Family

The Scariest Words Known to Man

I'll tell you what scares men. When the preacher says, "till death do you part." Those are the scariest words a man can ever hear. We can take "to love and to cherish" or "to have and to hold." But "till death do you part" sounds like a long, long, *long* time. Why not until my car breaks down? Or until I run out of money? Or until her ass gets too big?

God gave women something that he didn't give men: a heart. For women, relationships are built on emotions and feelings. They're more mature and not as superficial as men. The proof? I've seen plenty of pretty women with fat, bald-headed men. And as long as this man treats her right, she'll stay in love with his big, bald-headed ass. Be hugging all over him, just happy to be around him. Me? If my wife got fat and bald? I'm out like a scout on a new route. I'd be in court, saying, "Yes, your honor, she's a good woman, a fine woman. Takes care of me and my children and has a heart of gold. But look at her! She looks like Sherman Hemsley."

The Out Clause

While I am committed to being married, I do want to know what the out clause is. I'm trying to find the loophole. I play this little "what if" game with my wife:

Me: Hey, baby, what if, just hypothetically speaking, what if you found out I was cheating on you? Would you stay with me?

My Wife: Yeah, I guess. Unless I saw you with her, then I'd kill you both.

Me: Okay, that ain't it.

One time I was digging way down in the bottom of the "what if" barrel:

Me: Baby, here it is. I think I got it. What if I'm walking across the street, right, and a big Mack truck comes and . . . *POW* . . . knocks my legs and arms off. Would you stay with me then?

My Wife: *(without batting an eye)* Yes.

This one messed me up. If the shoe was on the other foot, even if the other foot was out on the freeway or something, would I be man enough to stay? Now, of course I'd have to stay for a little while. It'd be too cold-blooded to show up at the scene of the accident saying, "Hey, baby, how you doing? Ah, look, its just not gonna work out with me and you. Now, I done packed up all your shit . . . your legs are in the bag . . . got both your feet . . . oh, I don't know what this is, I think it's your baby toe. I'm gonna put that in the bag, too. Open your mouth . . . here's a little money. Buy yourself a skateboard and you be happy."

I'm talking more about as time goes by, as the years roll on, would I be able to hang in there and be supportive? Probably not. I'd probably start by trying to make her feel guilty about me staying. I'd walk around the house saying things like, "Yeah, I'd sure like to go out dancing. Haven't run a mile in a long time. I'd sure love to buy a trampoline."

I don't know if I'd even be able to get in the same bed as her. If one of those cold nubs rubbed up against me in the middle of the night, it would freak me out. I'd jump out of the bed, and say, "Girl, you gonna have to put some socks on or somethin'. I'm gonna have to get you some booties."

No, really, I'd stay. I love my wife. I'm here forever. I would even make love to her without the legs. Might be easier without legs. Sometimes the legs get in the way. You can do tricks with no legs. Put her on that skateboard, roll her ass into the bedroom, then throw her up in the air and spin her around on my dick. That way I'd turn a negative into a positive and we'd all have fun.

Running Out of Things to Say

I respect anybody that can stay married for a long period of time, because marriage is giving two hundred percent of yourself and not expecting anything in return except for some love. It's hard to please somebody physically, emotionally, and sexually for the rest of your life. And, believe me, I'm no superman. My wife still wants me to talk to her in bed. When we first got together, I could say things like, "You have beautiful eyes," and "I love making love to you."

Now that we've been together for seventeen years, I'm running out of things to say. Last night it was, "I like the way you stack the groceries in the freezer. The meats provide a real good foundation for the bulky bags of frozen vegetables, and then the way you balance the ice cream containers on top of it all. It really turns me on!"

How to Make Your Man Not Forget Your Wedding Anniversary

After all these years of being married, I'm realizing that I don't make the same effort that I used to in the romance department. This is messed up because my wife really deserves it. Sometimes I'll be watching TV and she'll walk into the room and I just get overwhelmed with love and appreciation for her.

I'll look over at her and say to myself, "Damn, look at this woman. I've known her almost eighteen years. She's given me four beautiful and healthy kids and she's still looking good. I need to go over there and tell her how much I love her and how much I need her in my life."

But then the commercial's over, the game's back on and I'm like, "Ahh, I'll tell her later. . . . Jordan's got the ball!"

Things had gotten to a point where we just had an anniversary recently and I almost forgot! It wasn't until she said "Happy Anniversary" that I remembered. I felt real shitty and selfish. I pondered and asked myself "Why?" Why did I forget? Even more, why do men in general forget? I've had friends who've forgotten their anniversaries. It's unforgivable, yes, but there's got to be a reason for it. And now, I think I've figured it out.

If you're a woman, I know what you're thinking—your man doesn't love you. But it's not that at all. It's because anniversaries are a celebration of the wedding ceremony. And the wedding ceremony was something dreamed up by the girl. That was y'all's little day on the town. The rice, the flowers, and all your girlfriends . . . Men didn't have any input into that. We just wanted to get laid and got tricked into all of this other stuff that in our minds is really just beside the point.

Let me illustrate my point:

Man: Hey, look, baby, I got to have sex with you or I'm gonna explode.

Woman: No, if you want me, it's going to be forever. Now, what you need to do is drop down on one knee and confess your love to me. Tell me that it's me and no one else and then I want you to give me a diamond ring to show me you mean business. And I mean a bigger diamond ring 'cause this little piece of shit you gave me for my birthday ain't working.

Man: Then am I gonna get some sex?

Woman: No, not yet. First, what we're gonna do is have this big celebration, and we are going to invite all my friends and family and everybody that you hate. And we are gonna congregate in church and in front of God and my father you are going to confess your love to me and you're gonna tell me till death do you part you'll love me and only me.

Man: Then can I get some sex?

Woman: No. Then we're gonna run out into the limo.

Man: We gonna have sex in a limo?

Woman: No, we're going to the airport.

Man: We gonna have sex on a plane?

Woman: No, we're going halfway around the world to an exclusive little island infested with mosquitoes. Then you gonna pick me up and carry me across the threshold and tell me how beautiful I am and how much you love me.

Man: Then we can have sex?

Woman: No, silly, I'll be on my period by then!

So you can clearly see why a guy can forget his anniversary. Ladies, if you wanted your man to remember your anniversary, you should let the men come up with the wedding ceremony. We would have come up with something that we would never forget.

Consider this alternative scenario:

Man: All right, girl, before I get all sentimental, this is what I need you to do. I want you to drop down on one knee and suck my dick like it ain't never been sucked before so that I know that it's you I want sucking my dick for the rest of my life.

Woman: Then you'll confess your love to me?

Man: No. Not just yet. First we're gonna have this big ceremony, and we gonna invite all of your friends—all of the fine ones, none of those fat bitches. They're gonna be dressed up in those little bridesmaid dresses with no panties on. I'll be wearing my all-white Nike sweatsuit, my Air Jordans on—unlaced. You'll be in white, too—an all-white bra and G-string panty set so my boys can get a good look at the ass that I'm getting for life. Then we will walk down the aisle while they're singing my wedding song, "Here comes pimp daddy. Here comes pimp daddy." I'll put my hand on your ass and look at your father like, "Yeah, what's up, Mr. Man? This is mine now!" Then the preacher gives us our vows, you say, "I do," and I say, "Till death or another woman do us part." Then he'll pronounce us man and wife.

Woman: And then you'll confess your love to me?

Man: No, not just yet. We got to have sex in the limo first. But before we leave I snatch off your G-string and throw it over my shoulder, and whichever one of my boys catches it gets to have sex with two of the bridesmaids.

Woman: Then you'll confess your love to me and say we'll be together forever?

Man: Well, that depends on how freaky you get in the limo.

See, men would never forget a wedding like this. They would actually want to renew their vows every month or so. Guys would be walking around whistling and smiling at strangers.

Man 1: Yo, man, why you so happy?

Man 2: It's my anniversary, dawg. I can't wait!

Talking Nasty to Your Wife

You don't want to live out your fantasy with your wife. A friend of mine once said, "Why can't he get freaky with me? I'm his wife. Why does he have to go outside of our relationship? I can be just as freaky."

The reason is every man wants to believe that his wife is a good girl. In bed, you don't want to talk to your wife like she's a prostitute, at least not for an extended period of time.

Imagine him saying, "Take that, you nasty ho. You like that, you dirty freak? Ya mama ain't teach you nothing, did she, you stank bitch!"

After a while, the man is going to start thinking, "Damn, I married me a stank ho! I've got to find myself a good girl."

It's a good thing women don't talk to their men like that in bed. Our egos just couldn't handle it. Imagine your woman saying, "Oh yeah, come on, ya fatherless faggot. Oh yeah, sling that little pencil dick. Hurt me, tiny balls!" You'd be in therapy.

If Your Wife Doesn't Like Your Friends, Watch Out

Women have enormous power over men, including whether or not you should keep a friend. Thing is, they'll achieve this without actually telling you to drop him. My wife is a master at this.

Wife: Where are you going?

Me: Just going to meet up with Preach at the bar.

Wife: You're gonna hang out with him?

Me: Well, yeah, that's my boy. We grew up together. why?

Wife: He gives me the creeps.

Me: What do you mean, the creeps?

Wife: I don't know. It's something about the way he looks at me makes me feel really uncomfortable.

Me: Uncomfortable like how?

Wife: No, that's your friend. I'm sorry I even said anything. You go on and be with him. I'm don't want to come between y'all.

When I finally meet up with Preach I got an attitude. I sit down and stare at him for five minutes without saying a word. Preach can feel all the tension.

Preach: Hey, man, everything all right at home?"

Me: Why are you so concerned about what's going on in my house? You trying to bang my wife?

Preach: Damon, what are you talking about? We've been friends for ten years!

Me: I know what you're up to, man. You're one of them creepy motherfuckas that be looking at his friend's wife behind his back. Get the hell away from me. And stay away from my wife before I kill you! You damn creep!

Me, Not Communicate?

My wife's number one complaint with me is that I don't know how to communicate. Can you believe this? I want to know what the hell I've been doing for the past eighteen years, talking to myself?

I think what she means is I don't sit around crying with her. I try to explain to her that a man communicates with actions. If I keep a roof over your head, food on the plate, car in the garage, diamonds on your fingers, Guccis on your feet, that's my way of saying "I love you." That's what I'm communicating. I don't do that for no other woman. I love you, and you should know that.

Now, if I was unemployed and broke, then I should have plenty to say. I should be writing poetry and singing songs about all I want to get you, but I can't get you because I'm too busy communicating with your silly ass.

Marriage Counselors Suck

I hate marriage counselors. This is the biggest scam in the world. Someone figured out a way that women can do the things they love best at the same time: talk and spend money. So they said, "Let's charge them one hundred an hour to force their husbands to sit and listen to them." But all the husband can think about is how much money he's spending, so you never have his complete attention:

Doctor: Mr. Johnson, did you hear what your wife said?
Man: Yes, I heard what she said. She says the same shit at home.
Doctor: Well, how do you feel?
Man: I feel like I should get a rebate.

It's amazing how polite everyone becomes in front of the counselors. It's like you're trying to impress him as a couple. Your mannerisms change. Every answer begins and ends with a "yes, honey," or "no, sweetie pie." You start wondering why you are there in the first place. Till you get to your car and start calling each other your other pet names, like, "bitch" and "motherfucka."

All the counselors think about is how they can extract more money from you. Their intentions are to get you separated from each other and convinced that you need some individual counseling, in order to work on personal issues. Sounds like a lot more hundred dollars in his pocket, doesn't it? And if kids are involved he'll tell you that they need counseling, and so will the dogs and cats, and you can't forget the fish because they are affected by the breakup, too. My advice: Work out your own problems so that money problems don't become another one of your problems.

Sneaking It In

There was a period in my marriage when I took my wife for granted sexually. The problem was, it was there all the time. I'd come home from work late, and she'd be in the bed with just a T-shirt and panties on. She was so tempting and sexy. I'd just roll her over and push it in. No foreplay—getting it in was the foreplay.

Sometimes she'd be sleeping and I'd have to sneak it in. I'd inch her drawers down. Just enough to get some room to maneuver. If she stirred, I'd softly sing to her, "Rock-a-bye, baby, on the treetop..." Because I didn't want to have to "make love." I just wanted to get it off. It wasn't always easy, though. I mean, sometimes she'd turn over, and I'd have to get up out of bed, walk around to the other side, and get started all over again.

If I got caught, though, it wasn't funny. In the morning she'd give me that look, as if to say, "You could have at least pulled my panties back up. My ass was freezin' last night—thanks to you, Quickdraw."

Making Love to Free Willy

One of the weirdest experiences you can have is making love during the pregnancy. You'll do it to try to keep the peace in the house, but there's really nothing erotic about it. 'Cause your wife will swell up. Everywhere—stomach, feet, hands. I'm talking Free Willy.

By the ninth month, my wife gained forty pounds and I barely recognized her. First couple of months it was cool because I psyched myself out. I'd look down at her stomach and think, "Maybe she had a couple of beers or something." But those last couple of months, she got so big she'd have to rock just to get up out of chairs. She'd wobble toward me and say, "Make love to me ... What's the matter? You don't find me sexy anymore?"

I'd say, "Have you seen your drawer size lately?

"That's okay," she'd say, panting. "We'll use them as a sheet. Come on, make love to me."

Well, a man's gotta do what a man's gotta do. I'd tell her to go into the bedroom and turn off the lights. Then I'd go into the bathroom with porno magazines, trying to get it up.

She'd get a little impatient waiting. "Damon, are you coming in here or what?!"

I'd say, "All right, baby, hold on, I'll be right there. Just let me see what it's supposed to look like."

The Delivery Room Is No Man's Land

I don't think a man should be in the delivery room when his wife is giving birth. It's very selfish on the woman's part to want him to be there, subjecting him to the same pains she's having. If the woman would take a second and think about it from the man's perspective, she'd understand what I'm talking about.

The guy's standing there next to his wife, doing his duty. He's breathing with her, holding her hand, giving her ice chips, encouraging her. That's fine. Suddenly his wife's vagina opens up and something the size of a watermelon pops out. He's going to freak out, seeing it get all abused. How's he ever gonna eat that again? That's like going to McDonald's and watching somebody spit on your hamburger, throw in on the floor, kick it around, and then serve it to you—you ain't never gonna eat there again.

On top of that, a man will feel very insecure about himself. I think that's why a lot of men faint in the delivery room. It's the shock of knowing that she was faking all those moans. My wife screamed and moaned with this eight-pound baby like she's never screamed and moaned before. I mean, it was for real. There's just no way my dick (which I haven't figured out how to weigh yet) could get even close to doing the same thing to her.

Anyway, the baby came out with this coat of stuff on it. I didn't know what it was. I was afraid to touch the baby. My wife actually wanted me to catch him. Yuck! I couldn't do it. Poor guy was hanging by his umbilical cord waiting on me because . . . I fainted.

Your Kids Will Ruin Your Sex Life

I thought that after I got married, I would be able to stop masturbating. Right after the wedding I said to myself, "Damn, I'm married now. I don't need to jerk off anymore." Then about two weeks later, I said, "Damn, I'm married now. I need to jerk off!"

But, really, sex was never a problem until my wife and I had kids. Before them, we'd do it anytime, anywhere, anyplace, and with anything—we were porkin'!! That's how we got four kids. My wife would be cooking dinner and I'd walk up behind her and say, "Hey, baby, what you doing? Looking all good, come here." Then I'd pull up her skirt and start hitting it. We'd get creative, doing it all over the kitchen, on the floor, on the table, even get her ass on top of the refrigerator. It was aggressive sex, wild, with all kinds of hollering and yelling and moaning. We were so noisy we'd set off car alarms.

It isn't like that anymore. The kids are always around. Now it's like a race and we're there playing that game Red Light, Green Light. I put it in and start counting, "Red light, green light, one, two, three," hoping to get done before any of the kids come in and catch us.

Now we got to act like we aren't doing it. We'll be in the bed on a Saturday morning, just rubbing, and one of my boys will walk in.

"Good mmmmmorning s-son. You need help with your homework? Grrrrrrreat! Why don't you go get your stuff and I'llllllllll m-meet you in a fffffew minutes? What am I doing? Ahhhhh, nooothinnnng. Jussst keeeeepin your mammmaa warrrgggghhhh, warmmmmmmmm."

Sometimes the kids affect my sex life without them even knowing it. I come home from work horny, ready to have sex. I'd walk up on my wife, and go to kiss her.

Wife: Get off me. You need to go talk to your damn kids, 'cause they are getting on my damn nerves. You better talk to them.

Me: Okay, baby, I'll talk to them. Now come here and give me a kiss.

Wife: No. I'm not in the mood, get off me.

Me: What did I do?

Wife: You look just like them. That's what you did. Now get off me, 'cause I am tired of all of y'all's shit.

Finally, I'd wear her down and we'd be having sex, but she'd still be complaining.

Wife: I told that little daughter of yours that if this is the attitude she's taking to school . . . Wait, move it to the left . . . yeah, right there. Anyway, I told her I will not accept these kind of grades . . . faster . . . because your father works too hard . . . wait, slow down . . . for you to not to be cooperating. What's the matter, Damon? Are you having problems at work?

Aerobics Are Not Good for a Marriage

My wife used to teach aerobics. I'd watch the results come home and I'd think to myself, "All right, I hope you're ready to carry some more kids." She wasn't happy about getting pregnant with our fourth child, but it was her fault, walking around the house looking all good. I'd look at that ass, and I'd say, "Take that, girl, see you in nine months!"

She kept inviting me to see her teach, but I never made the class. It's not that I wasn't proud of her or didn't want to be supportive. It's just I can't stand in a room filled with titties and ass and watch them bounce around and pretend like I don't see anything. If I go to her class, I can't be disrespectful and look at other women. I got to look her in the eye the whole time.

And these days women come in the gym with virtually nothing on. They have a sticker over each nipple and a string up the ass and that's the outfit. Then the exercises they do are very suggestive and the music they play sounds like porno. And my wife will be saying things like, "And up, and down, and in, and out . . . Up, and down, and in, and out . . . And spread your legs . . . hold . . . release . . ." I figure, halfway through this class, I'm gonna have my dick in my hand, and she ain't gonna be happy about that.

Father v. Son

My oldest son, Damon, just turned sixteen. It's scary seeing him grow up. The boy's tall, got big feet. And you know what being a teenager means. He's playing with himself. Now I have two masturbators in the house—and one of us has got to go! See, I know he's doing it because the boy spends most of his time in the bathroom. He comes home from school looking real sad.

"Hey, Damon, how was your day?" I ask.

He looks real unhappy and doesn't say hi or anything. He just makes a beeline straight to the bathroom. Then he comes out five minutes later all relaxed, with a big smile.

"Oh, hi, Dad," he says, all bright and cheery, trying to shake my hand.

"Boy, I don't want to shake your hand!" I mean, I want to be supportive and all that, but there's a line I just can't cross.

Knowing what it's like to be jerking off in the bathroom at that age, I really enjoy messing with him. I play with the doorknob when he's in there.

I'll knock on the door, saying, "Hey, Damon, everything all right in there?"

"Uh, yeah, Dad, everything's fine. I'm almost done." His voice is all nervous.

But I'll keep on, trying to throw his rhythm off, "Can I get you anything—some toilet paper, some lotion?"

One day, I'd like to do something really mean but it'd be fun—kick the door open and not even acknowledge what he's doing. I'll just say, "Wash your hands, it's time to eat."

He'll come to the table, embarrassed and uncomfortable. I'll just sit there and stare at him. Then I'll say something like, "What's the matter, you're not gonna eat your sausage?"

It's such an awkward age for him. He's growing so fast, and now he's even big enough to start wearing my clothes. He's so insecure about his size. His hands go past his knees, so he keeps them inside his pockets so his arms look normal. His voice is changing and cracking. And he's got three hairs on his nuts. He kinda has to jerk off, just to build self-esteem. He just abuses it, though. Anytime there's something he can't handle, he goes to play with himself.

"Spaghetti *again*? I'll be right back," he'll say, marching off to the bathroom again.

I feel bad for him because he has started something that he's never going to be able to stop. Once you start playing with your knob, you're in it for life. You'd think with technology as advanced as it is, they could invent something to help you to stop jerking off. They have a patch that you put on your arm and it stops you from smoking. Why can't they invent a patch you put on your nuts that can relieve stress and keep you from jerking off? They can call it Dickatine. It simulates an orgasm when you get stressed out.

Then when you get into a car accident and you jump out of your vehicle all upset.

"Man, what's wrong with you? This is a brand new car. I ought to beat your motherfu—"

And then the Dickatine kicks in:

"Oh my God . . . oh damn . . . hold up . . . hold up . . . don't touch me, don't touch me oh damn . . . aaaaarrrgghhhhhaaaahhahiahaiaiagyyahyyya . . . Hey man, I'm sorry, it's just a car. . . . Look, can I offer you a patch?"

They can't really invent anything like that because it would become the new drug on the street. There would be patch houses all across America. Neighborhoods would declare war against them. Self-righteous leaders would say, "These patch houses are ruining our community and we're not gonna . . . oh God, oh shit. Don't touch me! Aarrrhggaghajumba-layashuckakakakakahhgg . . . Oh man. What the hell was I talking about? Let those kids have their fun. I need a cigarette."

He-Man

I remember the last time I got high I realized that smoking herb makes you stupid. I was sitting in the living room looking at my three-year-old son, who was watching his favorite show, called *He-Man*, which is a cartoon that's kind of like Hercules. Little Damon had a sword in his hand and was running around the house with his diaper hanging down, screaming at the top of his lungs, "By the power of Grayskull, I have the power!"

After about twenty minutes of watching him run around, the only thing that I could think to do was trip him as he ran past me. The poor kid got up off the floor and looked at me as if to say, "What's wrong with you, asshole? What the hell are you doing? You broke my damn sword and put a hole in my diaper. Now there's shit all over the place. You happy now? You clean it up, 'cause I'm not. I'm gonna go tell Mama. Damn, I wish I was He-Man, I'd bust your stupid ass."

No Cussing in the House

With four kids, I've had to make sacrifices. Like, I can't curse in my own house. This may not seem like a big deal, but when you've got kids that make you want to curse, it really is a burden. Still, I watch my mouth in my house because kids say what you say, not what you don't say, and they're so incredibly impressionable.

I took my oldest son, Damon, to the movie *Home Alone* when it first came out. After we got back to the house, this fool went and put Krazy Glue on the toilet seat, hoping to stick his little sister to the bowl. This was his idea of a joke. I'm the one that took her to the bathroom, thank God. She was about two years old at the time. I removed her diaper and went to put her on the toilet. I looked down at the toilet seat, though, and saw the glue, and I was like, "What the fuck is this shit? Who the fuck put this shit on the toilet?"

My two-year-old daughter picked right up on this: "Fucking shit. Fucking shit is fucking shit . . . fuck this shit."

"Baby, don't talk like that," I said. "Daddy's sorry he said those bad words."

"Fuck that shit," was her reply. I'm glad my wife wasn't around.

I couldn't get mad at my son because it was kind of funny. I mean, I'm a comedian, and there's a rule in my house: If it's funny, you're not in trouble. The most I can say is, "Boy, work on your timing." If she got stuck on the bowl I would have had to laugh. Her behind is only the size of two nickels, so she has to hold onto the toilet seat to keep from falling in. Which means she would've got stuck hands and ass to the bowl. I would've had to take the whole toilet seat off and put that in the car like it's a car seat. Then, drive her to the hospital and I guess, throw her to the doctor like a Frisbee. He would've looked on in horror as she spun toward him saying, "Fucking shit. Fuck that shit. The fucking shit."

Laying Down the Rules

The greatest compliment to me as a father is when people like my kids. That makes me feel good. All the sacrifice and hard work is paying off. It would make me sick if people were talking bad about my kids, saying things like, "Oh, those damn Wayans boys are just trouble. They don't get any love at home. Just look at them playing in the traffic like that. It's a damn shame. Their parents need to be shot."

I believe as a parent you have to lay down rules and live by them yourself. I knew kids when I was growing up that could steal stuff and bring it home. My friend had a room full of stereo equipment that wasn't his and his mother would be in his room jamming to the music, saying, "Oh, baby, this is my song! Pee Wee, turn up the sound!"

I used to think to myself, "Damn, that stereo is stolen. And I know it's stolen because I helped steal it." That didn't happen in my house. If you didn't have a receipt, or couldn't justify where you got the money to buy the equipment, it didn't get past the front door. Being poor, we needed some of that stolen stuff, but there was no way I could bring it in the house. That taught me to work hard and appreciate the things I had. It kept me from being spoiled.

That's the worst thing you can do: spoil your kids. Take the Menendez brothers. Remember them? They killed their parents. How do you shoot your own mother and father? Apparently, there wasn't a lot of love in that house. But I think that a kid should understand that if you bring them into the world they have an obligation to, at least, let you live. I mean, parents feed you and clothe you. And I bet Mr. Menendez was the one who bought his sons their first guns. But they probably took it all for granted.

Thank God those boys are in jail. That's where they need to be. It's unfortunate for them that they didn't go to prison for killing their parents for no reason, because they would have gotten a lot of respect for that. Nobody would've messed with them. But they put it out in the trial that the father was molesting them. Now, that's the kind of stuff they want to hear about you when you're in prison. Bubba is gonna have them bent over with a girlie magazine on their backs, saying, "Just call me Daddy. I'm gonna make it feel like home."

You're the Proud Parents of a Baby Girl Named Monica

I feel sorry for the parents of Monica Lewinsky. I mean all those years of sacrificing, nurturing, and caring for their baby girl. All those late nights at the hospital, putting her through private school, and making sure that she feels loved and protected in the world. After all of that you end up being known as, "The Parents Who Raised the Ho."

It must hurt. I bet that before all of this happened Monica's parents were the biggest braggers in their town. You can just hear the proud father on the golf course, saying, "It's a government job with a great future. She has special security clearance. Mr. Clinton is crazy about her. Every night she brings me home a cigar from him. I just sit back and puff it thinking about how my little pumpkin is friends with the President of the United States. Do you know she can just walk right into the head office whenever she wants?"

You know now that the scandal is out in the open he gets shit from all those people he used to brag to, saying things like, "Hey, Lewinsky, certainly were right about your daughter and that 'head' office. Ha ha!"

Where's the Rule Book?

I'm raising four different personalities. I wish there was a rule book that you simply follow A-B-C, and you are guaranteed to raise a child that can function in society. But there's no such thing. You can feed them the same thing, send them to the same school, and dress them in the same clothes, and one will grow up to be a doctor the other one will be a crack addict. They are all so different. My daughters are low-maintenance, especially the older one. I can just talk to her and she'll understand exactly what I'm saying.

I can tell her, "Cara Mia, I'm really disappointed in you."

Her lower lip will start quivering and tears will well up in her eyes. "I'm sorry, Daddy. I don't want to disappoint you. I'm gonna go and punish myself." And she'll march right off to her bedroom.

That doesn't work on my sons. If I tell my son, "Damon, I'm really disappointed in you," he'll reply, "Well, you're gonna be real pissed off when you see the rest of the shit I did. You're about to be livid, old man!"

My youngest son, Michael, is growing up nicely. I'm glad, because I was worried about him for a while. He was spoiled as a baby and that made him a whiner. The boy would whine about everything. He would fall on the floor crying and throw these temper tantrums, and I would be thinking, "What the hell am I raising here?" He made me want to grab him and shake him and say, "Look, faggot, stop it!"

They say you shouldn't hit your kids. Obviously, whoever said that didn't have kids. I believe that you shouldn't hit *some* of your kids. Some kids, all they understand is an ass whupping. If I wanted to motivate Michael I'd have to pop him upside his head. I tried talking to him, reasoning with him, being a patient, understanding father, but he'd always frustrate me to a point where I'd have to hit him.

Me: Michael, would you go in there and clean up your room, please.
Michael: *(whiny)* Do I have to? I'm watching the Power Rangers.
Me: Yes, turn that television off. Your room is a pigsty and I want it cleaned.
Michael: *(more whiny)* Awwww, can't someone else do it?
Me: No, it's your room. Now, I'm not gonna tell you again, Michael. Go clean it up!
Michael: *(as whiny as a human being can possibly get)* But I don't want to! Why do I always ha—
Me: *Smack!*
Michael: Oh, you mean clean the room!

Suddenly, he turned into a little janitor. He got a big set of keys, a broom in his hand, and a squeegee in his back pocket.

Michael: *(singing)* Clean and shine, clean and shine.

My Son Is a Nerd

My two sons go to private school. It's a good one, the kind where if you lose your wallet, they return it with a note and a dollar that says, "Hope you weren't inconvenienced." The only drawback about private school is that my son, Damon, is a little nerd. My son will walk into my living room when I have my friends over. "Morning, Dad, can I borrow your computer? I want to do some extra-credit homework."

"Yo, slow that up, son. I got company. Put your hands in your pockets and be cool."

"Never mind, Dad, I'll just work it out in my head!"

That's my boy! I don't mind. I'd rather he be a nerd that becomes a doctor than some cool mother-fucka in jail. I'll have to go visit his cool ass on death row.

"Hi, I'm here to see Ice Wayans."

"Yeah, Ice . . . Sorry, it's too late," the guard would say.

"That's terrible! But was he cool?"

Disneyland: White Man's Paradise

Ilearned that you shouldn't promise a child anything unless you're going to follow through on it. It's better to say no because they will hold you to your word. I remember once I made the mistake of promising my kids two weeks ahead of time that I was going to take them to Disneyland, and they drove me crazy for two weeks straight. They would startle me out of my sleep, scaring the hell out of me.

Kids: Daddy, Daddy, Daddy!
Me: Wha— what is it? Is the house on fire?
Kids: Are we still going to Disneyland?
Me: Yeah, we're gonna go to Disneyland.

They got so caught up in it, they even made up a little song that they'd sing while they were marching around the house: "Daddy's gonna take us to Disneyland, Disneyland, Disneyland. Daddy's gonna take us to Disneyland in just one more week and six days, twelve hours, four minutes and eight seconds."

I'd be on the toilet and they would start banging on the door.

Kids: Daddy, Daddy!

Me: *(straining)* Wwwwwwwwhat?

Kids: Are we still going to Disneyland?

Me: Yyyyyyes . . . we gonna gggggo to Disneyland!

Then, they would be holding their noses, singing their Disneyland song, "Daddy's gonna take us to Disneyland, Disneyland, Disneyland. Daddy's gonna take us to Disneyland, as soon as he finishes in the potty!"

By the time we arrived at Disneyland I had an attitude. I really don't like that place. They charge a $32.50 fee just to get into the park, and they give you two dollars off for the kids like they're doing you a favor. And the place is always packed, mostly with white folks. They don't seem to have a problem paying the $32.50. It's like they're hypnotized when they're standing at the ticket office window.

A typical white person will say, "Why, Disneyland is the greatest place on earth. Here, Mickey, take my wallet and you give me back how much you think I should have."

Black people won't have any of that. They'll be at the gate arguing, "$32.50 to get up in this motherfucka? What, is Snow White gonna blow me during the electric parade? No, I just want to know when the $32.50 is gonna kick in. Let me tell you something, for $32.50 I'm gonna fuck one of them dwarfs. That's right, Dopey is gonna be real sleepy and grumpy tonight."

But Disney knows that a parent will pay anything to see their kids smile. That's how they get you. They could charge three hundred dollars and you'd be out there robbing banks trying to scrape the money together.

Parent: *(holding a gun)* All right, everybody freeze! Put your hands up, and nobody will get hurt. I just want to get my kids some mouse ears!

Taking Revenge on the Family Dog

I hate dogs. I hate them because they're nasty. I don't understand people who'll share their ice cream cone with a dog. I've watched dogs lick their balls, not just one time a day, but they lick them all damn day long. I bought a dog for my kids and the dog would lick his balls and then lick my kids in the face. I tried to get the dog to stop doing this, but he wouldn't stop. It was like a little game with him. Then, the dog started trying to do this to me. That couldn't continue.

One day I got fed up and decided to teach him a lesson. I stuck my finger up my ass and rubbed it on the tip of his nose. I said if he wants to be nasty, I'll be nasty, too. The dog was running around the house like he had gone mad. I chased him around with that finger until the message sank in: Don't lick your balls and then lick me.

Appreciate Your Parents or Die

Sometimes after we grow up we forget what it was like for our parents and all the sacrifices they made to take care of us. Some of my brothers and sisters have chips on their shoulders. They sit around saying things like, "Daddy didn't spend enough time with me."

And I'm thinking, "Daddy had three jobs to raise ten kids. You think he enjoyed himself, being away from home all that time?" I say be happy you're alive and be grateful you had a daddy who stuck around and didn't run away from his responsibilities. If my kids ever say that to me, I'll kill 'em.

Kid: You didn't spend enough time with me, Daddy.
Me: *POW!* Good. Now I don't miss you.

I spend a lot of time on the road, doing standup or doing TV work or on-location for films. I have a feeling there's going to be a point in my life when one of my kids is going to tell me he doesn't think I was a good father. In anticipation of that, I bought me a video camera and I videotaped my kids. I don't go around doing what everyone else does—I don't tape my kids doing cute stuff like playing at the beach or blowing out birthday candles. Everything bad they do, I put on videotape, and I mean everything. Needless to say, I've built up a huge collection of clips. So when, say, one of my sons comes up to me and says I wasn't a good father, I'll be ready.

I'll say, "Well, you wasn't a good son. And I have videotape to prove it. Go on, sit down. I've been waiting a while for this day, a long time. Let me put the tape in, turn on the TV. Okay, here we go. Now look, this is you when you hit your brother in the head with a hammer. See, I had to take him to the hospital to get that hook out of his head. Here's another one. These are my brand new suede shoes. And that's you dipping them in the toilet. Dip, dip, dip. Four-hundred-dollar shoes . . . just dipping them in the toilet. Now this is my favorite. This is me and your mother in the bed. Look . . . damn, that's pretty impressive. I can't do that move no more. See how happy I am? You see my face? All right, now look who comes in the room. That's you. You see my face now? Do I look happy to you?"

Po Me

I grew up *poor*. We were so poor we couldn't afford the other O-R. We were just PO. Sometimes we didn't eat because there was no food in the house. We'd ask, "Hey, Mom, what's for dinner?"

My mother would look at us and say, "Look, babies, there ain't no food in the house. We're having sleep for dinner. Now brush your teeth and get ready for bed. Keenen, you make sure everyone gets a little extra toothpaste tonight."

I felt sorry for my father 'cause he'd have to watch all ten of his children walk by him with that look that said, "Mr. Provider! Couldn't bring home the bacon. Couldn't even bring home a damn can of Spam. Thank God for water . . . You did pay that bill, I hope?"

I remember once I stole fifteen cents from my father and he missed it. You know you're poor when your father starts trippin' over change. He'd be stalking around the house, all upset: "All right, this ain't funny. Now, someone in this house took my fifteen cents! How am I supposed to pay the rent now? I want my money back. Otherwise, I'm gonna strip search every one of y'all, starting with your momma. One of the nickels was a buffalo head and that's worth at least six cents on the market. Come on now!"

Clubfoot

I was born with a clubfoot. I had to wear an orthopedic shoe with a heel about four inches thick, and it had a brace that went up around my knee, just like Forrest Gump, which caused me to limp when I walked. Thank God I lived in the ghetto because the people that didn't know me thought I was cool. They would say, "Hey, man, check out that brother's walk. He must be in a gang or something."

I used to get into a lot of fights, too, because kids used to tease me about my shoes. And I didn't like to fight. Actually, I couldn't fight, not even with girls. I had a fight with this girl in the sixth grade. I went through my preparations like Keenen taught me. I was doing my little boxing stances, motivating myself with things like, "Yeah, come on. This little bitch wanna fight me? Bring it on. Yeah, come on—bring it on!" When Elaine heard me call her a bitch, she went into this windmill stance and threw a barrage of punches at me—I've never been hit so hard, so fast, so many times. She had me running like a little bitch.

I guess you're not going to find too many handicapped bullies out there. You never hear a handicapped person say, "Give me your lunch money! Well, you better have it tomorrow, otherwise I'm gonna kick your ass."

And it's hard to imagine people being scared of a handicapped gang, running away, screaming, "Oh shit, run! Here come the Crips!" Then the leader rolls up in a low rider wheelchair saying, "Hey, punk, you got a problem with me? All right, then, don't make me get up."

Most of my fights were because of my mouth. We use to play this game called The Dozens. I was real good at this game because I was so insecure. Kids didn't want to play with me because they knew they couldn't talk about my shoe. If they did, then it'd turn ugly and the game was over. The game would usually go something like this.

Kid: Damon, yo mother is so fat she has to take her pants off just to get into her pockets.
Me: Yeah, well, your mother's so fat that when she gets on the scale it says, "To Be Continued."
Seymour: Yeah, well, your mother's so poor she can't even pay attention.
Me: Oh yeah, well, your sister is so ugly, they have to tie a pork chop around her neck so that the dog will play with her.
Seymour: Yeah, well, your mother is so black every time she goes to night school the teachers mark her absent.
Me: Hey, man, let's not talk about mothers, man. Let's just get off mothers, 'cause I just got off of yours.

Then, all the other kids would be laughing and trying to instigate a fight. This would usually provoke the kid to attack my disability.

Seymour: Yeah, so, so, so, what about the crippled people's shoes you be wearing? What about those, huh, huh?

That's when I would lose it. Something in my head would just snap and I'd go nonstop full-on frontal attack.

Me: Oh, you want to get real now, huh, Seymour? How about when your father ran out on your mother and left her with six kids, that's why two of your sisters have illegitimate kids, 'cause there's no one there to guide them. That's why one of your brothers is a junkie and the other one is a homosexual and that's why your mother's a prostitute, 'cause she can't afford to feed y'all. That's why when welfare comes over y'all gotta hide over my house 'cause you're trying to get two welfare checks and you're only supposed to get one. That's why you can stay outside so late 'cause nobody loves you at home. You ain't been hugged since you was a baby. And you're gonna grow up to be just like your father who you hate 'cause he's a loser. Okay . . . your turn.

POW! The game would usually end with a punch in my mouth.

Open Wide

Out of all of my brothers, I'd say Marlon has got the biggest mouth. And that's saying a lot, believe me. I remember once when Marlon was younger, he got into an argument with some kid. Marlon was all up in the boy's face telling him that he was going to kick his ass. Then, all of a sudden, the little kid spit right in Marlon's mouth and ran away. It all happened so fast. Marlon couldn't even chase after him. First, he had to get over the initial shock of what happened. Then he had to try and get the boy's spit out of his mouth.

That's not right. You won't ever see Mike Tyson spitting in your mouth, unless he's trying to bite your tongue.

My Last Hero

The worst day of my life was the day I watched my big brother Keenen get beat up by a white boy. Hell, he didn't just get beat up, he got beat down.

Keenen was into karate or "The Arts" as he called it, when we were young. And this white boy was talking shit about my brother's Chinese slippers that he used to wear, even in the snow. So, I went and told Keenen that he had to defend his karate shoes. I figured it was a win-win situation, and I'd enjoy seeing Keenen beat on the white boy.

Everybody in the neighborhood gathered in the building to see this fight. Bets were placed. Keenen was favored to win with a flying sidekick to this guy's nuts. But there's this thing in the ghetto where black guys feel they have to take off clothing before they can fight. It's supposed to show that they're mad. So, if a brother is ever standing in front of you butt naked, ready to fight, you'd better run.

Anyway, Keenen was in the middle of taking off his shirt when this white boy just hauled off and started whoopin' his ass. It looked like one of those hockey fights. Keenen couldn't even get one punch off 'cause his arms were stuck in his shirt. I wanted to help out, but I was in such shock because it all happened so fast. Before I knew it Keenen was lying on the ground in a bloody pulp with his shirt still pulled over his head crying.

I was yelling, "Get up, Keen! Use your nunchaku! Don't let him get away! Taste your blood like Bruce Lee did in *Enter the Dragon*! It will make you mad! Here, suck on your eye, it should make you furious! Get up, Keen, fight him! I know you can do it."

But Keenen just laid there, wounded and crying, telling me to shut up before he kicked my ass. I don't have heroes anymore. Everybody's an ass-kicking away from being humbled.

A Mother's Love

Mothers have the power to rescue their child in a time of need. Not just physically, but emotionally. I remember when I was in the seventh grade, I got caught making out with a girl in the assistant principal's office.

Okay, she wasn't just a girl, she was the town whore. Every school has one. You know, the girl who's overdeveloped and has no father at home. The only attention she gets is the boys in school that feel her up, even the handicapped ones. Well, this girl named Sharon had the biggest breasts I've ever seen, and the first ones I had ever touched. I'll never forget how warm they were. Felt like fresh-baked muffins. Anyway, she was one of these girls that pretended that she didn't like it. She would say, "No, no, no," while putting your hand down her pants. I got caught. The principal suspended me, and I had to bring my mother to school in order to get back in.

I was too embarrassed to tell my mother what had happened. So, I just said, "The teacher wants to see you." So, there I am, sitting in the principal's office with my mother seated next to me, and the guy is going on and on about me being a pervert. He was making me out to be the next Jeffrey Dahmer. I could feel my mother looking at me, even though I had my head down. I was so ashamed. And she felt that.

So, right in the middle of the principal's speech, my mother cut him off and said, "Look, don't waste my time with this bullshit. I can't help it if my son is a lover."

Right then and there, I fell in love with my mother. I looked over at her and she smiled at me. I thought to myself, "Yeah, I'm a lover." I felt good about myself. I actually told the principal, "Yeah, don't be wasting our time. I'm a lover, and I got some more lovin' to do. What's your wife doing later?"

My mother grabbed my hand and pulled me out of the office before I was a dead lover. When we got outside, she slapped the shit out of me, and told me if I ever did that again, she'd beat my Billy Dee ass with a billy club. I'll always love my mama.

A Mother's Love II

Mothers also keep things real.

When you do business with your family, things can get out of control sometimes. My sister submitted ten scripts for a show I was producing called *413 Hope Street*. I rejected them because they were . . . well, okay, they sucked. When something like this happens in the Wayans family, you can bet you're gonna receive a call from Mama Wayans.

Mom: Now, Damon, you mean to tell me that out of ten scripts that your sister sent you, you couldn't push through one of them?

Me: Mom, I have to put my name on this work. I can't just send out anything.

Mom: Well, you sent out *Blankman*. That was some bullshit if I ever saw some. Your name was on that, wasn't it?

Thanks, Mom.

Antoine

My mom and dad did have their hands full with the ten kids, especially when we were dating. My sister used to go out with this dude named Antoine. He used to speedball, where you mix heroine with cocaine and shoot it into your veins. Once he came by my house to meet my parents right after speedballing. He knocked on the door like he would never stop: *knock,knock,knock,knock,knock,knock,knock, knock,knock,knock,knockknock* . . .

When my father answered the door, Antoine was nodding out, digging in his butt.

"Aw, hey, hey, hey—what's happening, daddy-O?" Antoine said. "Oh, you gonna pass on the handshake? Oh, I'll just finish doing what I was doing then, I got a wedgie. Look, I'm here to pick your daughter up. I'm gonna take her to the movies. We gonna go see *Caligula*. Say, this is a nice place you got here, Mr. Wayans. This is all right for the projects. I especially like this color TV you got here. That's one of them Sony Trinatrons. What's that—a nineteen-inch? Let me ask you something, Mr. Wayans, about how much do that weigh?"

My dad was stunned speechless. Then my sister walked into the room.

"Oh, hey, what's happening, Diedre? Come here, give me a kiss. No, give me some tongue. I don't care if your daddy's watchin'. What you had for dinner? Chicken? I can taste that. Look, I was just talking to your pops. He has some sorta attitude problem. Oh, he's a preacher? Oh shit. Let me go talk to him. Excuse me, Mr. Wayans. . . . Look, I know you're concerned about your daughter. I understand the father-daughter relationship. I got five kids of my own. But I want you to know that I love your daughter. This is some good pussy right here. See, I've been through a lot of hoes in my day, and your daughter stacks up number one. I mean if your wife is half as good as Diedre in the bed, then I see why you got all these kids running around here. Give me five. Oh, you gonna leave me hanging. . . . Damn."

My mother came into the room to see what was going on. Antoine went right up to her.

"Oh wow, this must be your moms, Dee. The Queen Bee is in the house. How you doing, Mrs. Wayans?"

He tongue-kissed my mama's hand, and she pulled it back right away.

"My name is Antoine. I'm French, as you can see. Now, I see where Diedre gets her big ass from. That's your genes, huh? Yo, Dee, what's wrong with your mama? What do you mean, I offended her? All right, look. I'm gonna apologize and get out of here. Excuse me, Mr. and Mrs. Sensitive. Diedre told me I offended y'all poor niggers. You must forgive me. I'm a little nice, is all. I just shot up before I came. Anybody got some matches? I wanna light up this joint. Maybe it will take some of this tension out the room."

Hot Steaming Stinking Bad Breath

I got a little nephew in New York who I got out of the projects. Damien is a sweet eleven-year-old, but he's real tough and he acts like he's in his twenties. You bump into him and he may take your life. I have to hide my wallet from him when I know he's coming over, so I put it under the couch.

"Yo, what up, Uncle Damon?" he said when he came over last week. "How you livin'? You living large or what? Shit is lookin' lovely 'round here. Your shit is looking mighty fine."

I can't do the same cute kid stuff that I do with my son with him. For example, I wanted to take him to Disneyland. My nephew looked at me like I was crazy.

"What I want to see some swollen rat for? You want to do something with me? Take me to see *Pulp Fiction*. Yo, I love the way they be talking about them bitches. That shit is true. That shit is true."

I was going to buy him a video game 'cause my sons love 'em. Again, my nephew was offended.

"Yo, don't play me like a Spice Girl. You want to do something for me? You trying to show me some love and affection? You wanna say, 'Hey, I love you'?

This is what you can do for me. I saw this five-finger gold ring. I saw this seven-inch gold chain. I saw me a BMW 318i. You want to do something for me? *Do dat shit for me!* That's the way to my heart."

"You know I don't have no money like that, Damien," I said.

"Oh, you ain't got no money? You ain't got money like that? Uncle Damon, helloooo. I be seeing you on TV. I know you getting paid out the gluteus maximums. Okay, okay. All I find I keep."

"What?"

"You heard me. All I find I keep! 'Cause I know where your wallet is. Your wallet is right under the couch."

Like I said—he's a sweet kid. He just needs a little guidance. He got suspended from school for telling the teacher her breath stank. My sister got all bent out of shape. I told her not to spank him. He's just expressing himself. You can't beat him for that. I wish I could tell somebody that their breath stinks.

Have you ever talked to someone and their breath is just kicking? Just burning the hair out of your nostrils? But we are taught to be nice and to just stand there and take it. You try and be polite and offer them gum. And they say, "No, thank you, I don't chew gum."

And you're thinking, "That's why your breath smells like shit! Maybe you should try sucking on a piece."

We've all had a bad breath teacher. I had one named Miss Anonoff. Her breath smelled like hot garbage. She was my math teacher. It's always the teachers that have to talk the most that have the worst breath. She used to smoke cigarettes, drink coffee, and on her desk she had this block of cheese she would dip into. I guess the cheese was to seal the nasty smell in.

This lady would be all up in my face, trying to help me, her hot steamy breath stinking up my clothes, "Nooo, honey. That's wwwrong. What you want to dooo is carry the fffiive over the ttthree. Then multiply it by twooo."

"Look, just fail me," I said. "Give me an *F* and get the hell out of my face."

"Hhey, don't talk to me like that, young mmman," she said, bristling. "I'll call your mmmother."

That actually seemed like a good idea to me. "Yeah, just talk to her. She'll understand. Matter of fact, just write her a note and lick the envelope. She'll get it."

Seymour's Rotting Mouth

When it's your friend who has bad breath, that's a whole different story. For as long as I've known Seymour, he's had this horrible problem. He's so afraid of the dentist, he will let his teeth rot out of his mouth. When he has a toothache, I ask him why he don't go to the dentist and he'll just say, "'Cause the tooth is almost gone. Soon, there won't be any pain."

See, when we were young, we used to go to the community health center to get our teeth fixed. When you don't have money or insurance, they don't fix your teeth. They pull 'em. No matter how big or small the problem is.

Dentist: Oh, we're going to have to pull that out.
Seymour: But it's just a little chip.
Dentist: Yes, I see that, but it still has to go.
Seymour: Well, what about this other tooth with the coffee stain?
Dentist: Oh, that's gotta go, too.
Seymour: That can't be!
Dentist: Well, when you get some insurance, we'll talk about saving some teeth.

So, after dealing with that, Seymour never went back to the dentist. And now he has that halitosis. His breath stinks through his face. He doesn't even have to say anything. All you have to do is stand next to him, and you'll be like, "Hey, man, what's that rotting smell? *Damn!*"

When Seymour and I used to go clubs, I would always instigate trouble. I would try to get him to talk to girls just to watch their reactions. I remember one night when it was especially scary.

"Yo, Sey," I said while we were hanging out at the bar. "Check out that girl over there—she's givin you the eye."

Of course, she was the hottest woman in the club, and she was completely oblivious to him.

"Yeah?" he said, checking her out. He licked his lips, which is not a good thing.

"Yeah, man," I said, encouraging him. "She's scoping you out. Go over there and talk to her."

"How's my breath?" he asked me, giving me a whiff.

"Ahhhhh, it's cool, man, it's cool," I said, trying to keep my balance. It was getting hard holding my breath so I couldn't smell it and talk at the same time.

Seymour grabbed his drink; he thought the alcohol would kill the smell but it would actually intensify it. He walked over to the girl all cool:

"Hey, baby, what's up? Where you going? Come back. Don't run from me. Come back and talk to me. Damn, girl, why you in such a rush? What's all this blinking about, got something in your eye? Are you crying? Hey, why are your eyes rolling back in your head?! What the fuh . . . ? Oh, oh, now you gonna lay down on me, playing dead?"

Seymour returned, playing like he had a real shot at her. "Yo, Dee, man, I had it going on there a little while and then she passed out on me. I guess she just couldn't handle my shit!"

Part 3

Race

Black Reporters Got It Hard

Any time there's a disaster in the news, the black reporter gets that assignment. They never get the fun stuff—like the space shuttle launch, or the Oscars, or the Thanksgiving Day Parade. It's always a war or something where bullets are flying and people are dying. Remember when we had the riots in LA? There was nothing but black reporters out there.

Black Reporter: This is Leon Jackson! I'm standing on Normandie and Crenshaw. . . .
BLAM! BLAM! BLAM!
Black Reporter: Man they're shooting out here! It's getting pretty bad. They're looting everything, everywhere. . . . Hey, nigger get off me. . . . They got my camera. . . . Come back with my camera!

We had mud slides. The brother was buried up to his neck in mud.

Black Reporter: This is Leon Jackson—I'm swimming in, aggghhh, approximately twelve feet of mud. It's pretty, aggh-hahghh, bad out here as you can see. I'm not gonna be able to breathe in a minute. Aaagghh. Help!

Meanwhile, the white anchorman is always in the studio, safe and sound, trying to act concerned for the brother.

White Anchorman: Gee whiz, Leon, it certainly looks bad out there. Our hearts go out to poor Leon and his all-black crew. We're hoping that somehow he'll make it through this.

Then they try to interject some humor:

White Anchorman: Hey, Leon, don't get anything on that camera or your name will certainly be mud around here. Har har har.

A Haitian, a Plunger, and the NYPD

I love New York City. It's the only city where people pride themselves on "keeping it real." That means they're just plain ole rude and don't plan on apologizing for it. And there are times when some real mean things can happen. Like when some New York City cops got together and shoved a plunger up the butt of a Haitian man named Abner Louima. This happened about a year ago. When I heard about it my first thought was *ouch*. Then I was thinking, "Where did the cops get the plunger from?"

It's not like cops have plungers as part of their uniforms. If it were a ticket book, a badge, a pair of handcuffs, or maybe a doughnut up his ass, you would be able to say, well, the cops got mad and grabbed for the first thing they could find. But a plunger is so unusual. I think what happened was Mr. Louima didn't know the "nigger rule," which is, if you're black you don't talk back to cops. We have past examples (like Rodney King) of what could happen to you when you're trying to cooperate with the cops, let alone resist.

Mr. Louima, being from Haiti, probably thought he had some special privileges here, like freedom of speech. I can just picture him in the backseat of the police car yelling at the cops:

Louima: Ya can't treat me like this. I'm not black, I'm Haitian!

Cop: Hey, look, nigger, just shut your fucking pie hole back there!

Louima: Don't talk to me like that, I'm not black, I'm Haitian! Take me down to my embassy! I got rights!

Cop: The only rights you are going to have is this right hand going right across your face! You shut your trap! You want to talk shit to me, pal? You want to be a shit talker? Huh? I'll shove . . . a . . . a fucking . . . uh . . . plunger up your ass!

Louima: I dare you. I'll report you so fast it'll make your head spin! I'm not black, I'm Haitian!

Cop: *(to his partner)* Tommy, pull over to that hardware store right here!

They shoved that plunger deep in his ass, then stuck him to the wall.

Louima: For God's sake, get me down from here! I'm not black, I'm Haitian!

I want to know what made these cops think they could get away with this crime? Did they think they could just falsify the report and it would go unnoticed?

Cop: Ah, the suspect dhere tried to escape true the bathroom window. And after repeatedly falling on a plunger twenty-six times, we were finally able to apprehend him. P.S. He's not black, he's Haitian.

Racism? What Racism?

Brothers can't afford to get too comfortable in show business 'cause that's when you become their pawn. They use your ass. Any time white people want to show how wonderful the world has become, they go get that rich nigger and put his ass on TV to represent all black people.

Then they ask questions like, "Mr. Wilson, now that you've made thirteen million dollars on your last film—not that we're counting—let me ask you a question. I'm gonna throw it out there and you just respond any way you want—Is there racism in America?"

Now he's sitting there on national TV thinking about that paycheck and this is what comes out of his mouth, "No, sir, an ifin there is, I ain't seen nun."

White Sale

It amazes me that we can send men to the moon, make cell phones that are smaller than the human hand, yet we can't stop racism. I've come to the conclusion that it has to be about money. Hate generates big business. I believe the Ku Klux Klan, for instance, is just an excuse to sell sheets.

Klan Salesman: Hey, Jethro, you still hate that nigger 'cause he took your job?

Jethro: Hell, yeah.

Klan Salesman: Shit, you can't go hatin' no nigger in a pair of jeans. He's liable to see you hatin' him and kick your ignorant white ass. What you need is a disguise. You know what them niggers are scared of? Ghosts. Now, I got some sheets here that'll make you look like Casper. That's right, just $19.95 and I'll throw in a pillowcase for free.

Jethro puts the sheet on. He's happy.

Jethro: This is great! I'm gonna go scare me some niggers.

Klan Salesman: Just hold on a minute, there, boy. Where are you runnin' off to? You can't go hate no nigger with just a sheet on. He's liable to pull that sheet off your head and see you hatin' him and kick your ignorant white ass. What you need is a gun.

Jethro: Really?

Klan Salesman: Hell, yeah, boy. Now, I got me one of these here shotguns that sprays buckshot so far you can get the nigger and any of his nigger friends that's liable to take the gun away from you and kick your ignorant white ass.

Jethro: How much is this here weaponry?

Klan Salesman: For you? Only $49.95. Okay, now where you gonna find a nigger at?

Jethro: I don't know. Where do I find 'em? It's getting dark.

Klan Salesman: See, I knew you wasn't as dumb as you look. Now, what you need is a dog, boy. Not just any dog, you need a nigga-hunter. Now, this here dog I gots is kin to the very dog that caught Kunta Kinte. He's just $29.95 and I'm fixing to throw in this here Ku Klux Klan secret membership patch which makes you o-fficial.

Jethro: Thanks. I'll take him.

Klan Salesman: My pleasure. Y'all come back now, ya hear? And tell some of yo ignorant white friends.

White Boys

What is this obsession that white guys have with tits? They can be so creative when it comes to describing them.

White Boy: Hey, man check out those cones, man. You see those babies? They're titanic. No, they're bodacious, dude. They're like headlights, or door knobs, man. No, they're cow tits, twin towers, hooters, cantaloupes, one-eyed melons, bowling balls. Half moons, Neanderthals, softballs.

Black Guy: Yeah, she ain't got no ass, though. That's an ironing board. It's like a crack in a wall.

Another thing that makes me laugh about white guys is when they get upset. They can be so verbally aggressive, it's scary.

White Boy: That fucking guy over there pissed me off, man. I'm gonna stick my finger up his fucking nose and pull his goddamn head off his shoulders, then shove my cock down his fucking neck, that jerk-off, man.

Black Guy: Why don't you just fight him?

White Boy: Naw, man, I'm not into violence, dude.

Black Leadership

I wonder who the next real black leader is going to be. It seems that nobody wants to step up to the plate and try to fill the void. I don't think there is a real leader out there who would be willing to risk his life for the complacent black people who live in this country. I guess it's because part of the job description is you must be willing to get shot in the head to be a good leader. I don't blame them for being afraid. Any time someone starts talking pro black they're liable to get shot. Here are three speeches given by the next three black leaders.

October 3, 1999

Announcer: Ladies and gentlemen, I'd like to introduce to you a man who will lead us into the twenty-first century. He's a graduate from Harvard and received his doctorate from Columbia. He has been fighting for black people all of his life and now he's here to speak to us. Give a round of applause for the one and only Dr. . . . Troy . . . Watson. *(long applause with a standing ovation)*
Troy: Good evening, my beautiful black brothas and sistas . . . *POW!*

November 3, 1999

Announcer: Ladies and gentlemen, we have here today the late Dr. Troy Watson's younger brother, the Reverend Kevin Watson.
Kevin: Thank you. You know before my brother was shot down he said that black people need to unite. . . .
POW!

December 3, 1999

Announcer: Ladies and gentlemen, the second cousin of Kevin and Troy Watson, Cecil Watson.
Cecil: Hello.
POW, POW, POW!

So, now, all we have are the sell-outs. Their speeches are very accommodating.

Sell-out: Good evening, ladies and gentlemen. I'm here tonight to talk about racial harmony. Not of just black people but I'm talking total integration. One race, the human race. Black people need to know white people are people first, not the animals that they've been made out to be. They're just like us, except they got a lot more than we do. And that's okay 'cause we should be happy with the meal that's put on our plate. We have a lot of programs designed to ease our burdens that we don't fully take advantage of, like welfare, WIC, and the newly instituted "nigga don't work program." And if black people want more than that then they need to come together . . .
POW!

Al, Jesse, and Farrakhan

If you take a good hard look at black leaders today, there's not much out there. Things, in fact, look pretty bleak. Take Al Sharpton, for instance.

I must have been asleep the day they elected Al Sharpton as the black representative. He is the only leader in history to show up to a rally wearing a tight red velour sweatsuit. The suit was so tight that you could see his balls imprinted on the sides of his legs. It looked like he was hiding olives. I say, if you're gonna be the representative have a bigger set of balls than that.

And what's up with the brother's hair? It looks like he swallowed James Brown. One time he showed up to a rally with a roller in his hair. It wouldn't have been so bad if he was wearing a whole set of rollers 'cause we as black people can understand this, but no, not Al. He shows up with one big roller in the front of his head, looking like he's Wilma Flintstone. I'm not sure Al is what Martin Luther King, Jr., had in mind when he was imagining the future of black leadership.

Then there's Jesse Jackson. I just have one question for him: Why is he at every sporting event that ever takes place? I just saw him at the Tyson fight.

That's strange to me. You never saw the old civil rights leaders at basketball games, right? You never saw Martin Luther King at a Muhammad Ali fight yelling, "Kick his ass, kick his ass. By God Almighty, kick his ass!"

No, Martin had things to do. Marches to lead, rallies and speeches to give. He had an agenda. Jesse used to. But all that rhyming in his speeches diluted his cause. The last speech I saw Jesse give had everyone scratching their heads.

Jesse: It is a fact that we are under attack by people that stab us in the back simply because we are black. Now I must go pack, I will be back. Going to Iraq to meet up with Shaq and have a Big Mac attack. They'll be nick nack, no paddy wack. Or give a dog a bone like Macaulay Culkin who's home alone. Pick up his phone there's no dial tone.

But I am somebody who rocks the party. I am somebody who rocks the body-body.

Finally there's Minister Farrakhan, who to me is a very interesting black leader. I can't help but laugh when he speaks because he scares the shit out of white folks. He ain't trying to make friends in the white community. White people are scared of Farrakhan because he's such a passionate speaker who can get black folks riled up. His speeches are so powerful he can make black people stop celebrating Christmas.

Farrakhan: Christmas is the Devil's holiday. It started back in slavery where the white slave master would put on a red sheet and climb down the slave quarters' chimney. And just like the devil he was, he wouldn't get burnt by the fire. That's why they call him Santa because you take the N in Santa and put it at the end of Santa and you've got Satan Claus. Then he'd grab that slave out of the bed 'cause he knew when he was sleeping, and he knew when he was awake. He knew 'cause he owned him, for goodness sakes. Then, he'd castrate that slave and start singing "Jingle Bells." And when the slave's woman would protest, she'd get down on her knees and beg, "Please, Massa, don't take him. Let my man go." And the massa would look down at her with those beady blue eyes of his and say, "HO, HO, HO, go back to bed before we hang your black ass, too."

Africans v. Americans

I can tell you this, the next black leader is not going to be an African native. This may be hard to believe, but I've discovered that Africans don't respect black Americans. I was at a party and I met this African guy. I thought, "Cool. He's black, I'm black. He's from the mother country. There can be a real connection here." He wouldn't have any of that, though.

He said to me, "Why do you call yourself black? That means nothing. You are not black, you are a man, you are an American. You were born here, you are not African American. You are American, and that's it, asshole.

"I am African. My name is Kwanza. I'm from the jungle, baby, and I killed a lion when I was eighteen years old, beating him to death with my dick. That's a man! You are here in America kissing up to the white man. You are a slave. All you blacks here in America want to do is play basketball and sing the rap songs. You think that's the only way out of the ghetto? Just get a job, sucka. Do something that is going to make a difference. Me, I've been in the country two years, I'm already the manager of a delicatessen.

"I don't understand black faggots either. You kiss the white ass all day and then you go and suck his dick at night. What's wrong with you? Where I come from we don't have faggots, baby. We test every man. We take them out to the jungle and fuck them in the ass. If they like it, then we know and we kill them."

The Good Reverend

And I'm not sure you can find the right kind of leadership in church either. Thanks to preachers, a lot of people have given up on religion completely. Today, going to church is like going to Vegas. You'll leave thinking, "Man, I lost $75.00 up in this motherfucka."

Preachers give religion a bad name. But that's the people's fault. All they want is to go to church, sing a song, give five dollars and clear their consciences. You can't do that because that's when the preachers start taking advantage. He'll have you believing that the only way to righteousness is by paying for it. And there's nobody better at convincing people of that than the Honorable Reverend Edward Cash. His sermon goes something like this:

"Good Evening. Welcome to the *Hour of Power*. This is TV prayer and my name is the Reverend Ed Cash—dollar bills, y'all. I'd like to begin this evening's sermon with a few announcements.

"Last week someone put a food stamp in the basket. Now, I know I said give what you can. Yes, please give what you can. But y'all keep the food stamps. Go buy the baby some milk with that. 'Cause, see the Lord can't use no coupons. No, sir. They don't give out vouchers up in heaven. And we must keep in mind that this is the Lord's account. That's right, and the Lord got bills to pay, yes indeed. Ya wake up tomorrow there won't be no sun in the sky. No, sir. The Electric Man came and turned that off. Then who looks bad? The Lord looks bad. 'Cause He's keeping you in darkness. Can't get that light. Can I get an Amen? That's right!

"Now, there seems to be jealousy and envy in the congregation. And it's pointed at me. Sister Shepherd came up to me and said, 'Reverend Cash, you can't preach the Word because you drive a Rolls Royce.' She's looking in my backyard, ya see. She got her nose all up in my business. And I had to tell her, 'The Lord don't like ugly and you're fat and ugly so I rebuke you! You don't belong in church. You belong in Jenny Craig!'

"Yes, I drive a Rolls Royce. Yes, I do. But it's not my car. It's the Lord's car. I'm just His chauffeur. The Lord's in the backseat. I gotta take him around to where his spirit needs to be. Now, as I look out here at your faces, I see that some of you don't believe that I have the spirit. No, sir. You are non-believers. So I must prove to you that I have the spirit every week. Now some of you say, 'Well, how?' By speaking in tongues. A-hem . . .

"Al a weta. Al a weta. Jhon today tela vo. So ma loma tina. So mo loma tina. Ding Dong Ding. Ding Dong Ding. Donde esta y stades Bien gracias y tu Como esta les bibliotecqua.

". . . And I'm back. Sometimes the spirit just hits me and that's to let you know I'm full of it.

"Can I get an Amen?"

Nigga Business

When you're black and successful there are two types of black businessmen you have to deal with. There is a regular black businessman, that can meet with you, iron out an agreement, and stick by it. Most likely after everything is said and done, everyone will make money and all is well. Then, there's the nigga business. That's where you try to do a favor for someone and they try to make an ass out of you, treating you like they're doing *you* the favor. It goes something like this:

1: I call you and leave your mother a message saying I need a driver, and I want to meet you at 4:00 to talk about the particulars. You don't show up or call for a week because you had to get some pussy.

2: I hire you as a chauffeur anyway because you say you're my cousin. The first thing that comes out of your mouth is "Why didn't I get the six hundred like Puffy Combs got?" And then in the same breath you ask me if can you borrow my car so you can go and get more pussy.

3: Come Tuesday, you want me to pay you for the week and lie to unemployment and tell them you don't really work for me, so that way you can collect two checks a week because I'm making money, and you feel you should make money, too, so that you can get even more pussy.

4: Then I ask you to wash my car, and you get mad because you feel you shouldn't have to wash no damn car, especially since I ain't going to let you drive it so you can go get any parts of pussy.

5: I ask you to take me to a club to hear some music, and you tell me the club I want to go to ain't got no bitches in it. At least not the type you like. You want to take me someplace where we can get all the pussy.

No more nigga businessmen for me, thank you.

One-Night Stand

Last time I was in New York I stayed at a really nice hotel. One night I got back in late, walked through the lobby, and got on the elevator. I pushed my floor and stepped back, and this nicely dressed white woman got on, too. She pressed a button, then looked back over her shoulder in my direction and her eyes went wide. Just as the doors were about to close, the woman jumped out of the elevator. This scared the shit out of me, 'cause I thought there was an ax murderer in there or something. So I jumped off right behind her. But she thought I was stalking her, so she took off screaming through the lobby, which scared me even more, so I started running and screaming, too.

Handi-Man to the Rescue!

Sometimes I think about how bad black people got it, but there are people that have it worse then us. Like handicapped people. It gets quiet when you mention the word "handicapped" because it makes people think about that cousin they haven't seen in years.

But forget about that for now. Handicapped people don't have role models, though more than anyone else they really need them. I think they should have their own superhero, a paraplegic. That would be great. He could be called Handi-Man.

The show would open up with some funky music. Then the narrator would say, "Up in the sky it's a bird, it's a plane. It's a wheelchair. No, it's Handi-Man!"

Cut to the opening scene. A woman being confronted by a mean-looking thug.

Victim: Handi-Man, Handi-Man, help!

Handi-Man, cruising in the sky in his custom-made Super Duper Wheelchair, hears her.

Handi-Man: Uh-oh, it sounds like trouble.

Handi-Man flies down quickly and accidentally lands on top of some innocent bystanders who are just checking out the action.

Bystanders: Hey, watch the fuck out!!
Handi-Man: Excuse me. Hey, you, leave the lady alone.

The thug snickers and ignores Handi-Man, who staggers out of the wheelchair and cripple-walks closer.

Handi-Man: I said let the girl go or ya gonna have to deal with me.

The thug pulls a gun and shoots at him. Handi-Man, unfazed, continues toward the thug, who suddenly looks very frightened.

Handi-Man: You can't harm me anymore. I got Palsy. Put the gun down. I said put it down.

Handi-Man grabs the bad guy with his crooked finger and flips him. The thug screams and crashes into some garbage cans, passing out.

Handi-Man: That's right. Never underestimate the powers of the handicapped!

The victim runs over to Handi-Man and hugs him.

Handi-Man: Now, now, ma'am, everything's just fine.
Woman: Oh, Handi-Man, you're my hero!
Handi-Man: I guess I am. Would you help me back to my wheelchair? I can't feel my legs.

As the woman walks him to the wheelchair, the crowd chants, "Handi-Man! Handi-Man! Handi-Man!"

The End

Handicapped people don't need pity. They need heroes!

Interracial Couples

I don't understand interracial couples. In Hollywood, it's so common that brothers look right through black women. They'll be at a club and lean over to a black woman to say, "Excuse me, sistah, could you tap that white girl for me?"

I appreciate beauty, I really do. It's not that I can't recognize a pretty white woman when I see one—I see them all the time. It's just some brothas, though, have no discriminating taste. If they had a choice between a beautiful black woman and old white ho, they'd pick the whitey. They'll show up with any kind of girl as long as she's white. I'm talking about the white girls that white boys don't even want. Then they roll up on me all happy, like they struck gold.

Brother: Yo, Damon, what's up? I want you to meet my little snowflake here. Damon, this is Betty Lou. Betty Lou, this is Damon.

Me: Hi, Betty Lou, nice to meet you.

Betty Lou: Chits nacha ta meetch yarghah, toow.

Me: What'd she say?

Brother: Yo, chill, Dee. I met her down at the Special Olympics. Isn't she white? Yo, if you're interested, she got a friend in a wheelchair.

Part 4

Relationships & Sex

Mrs. King, Meet Mrs. Ghandi

The beauty of a woman is that she can love you unconditionally. I think about all the great men throughout history who've done great things, they've all had great women with them. They had women kicking them in the ass saying, "You can do it, baby. Go ahead, give it your best shot." A man needs that because then he knows he can fail, and always come back home. You think about Martin Luther King. If he didn't have a strong, supportive wife, he would've never been able to accomplish what he did. If Coretta Scott King was a nagging wife things would've turned out completely different for Martin.

He'd be leaving the house one day and she'd stop him at the door, saying, "What, are you going out marching again? This is the third time this week! You got all them brothers under your control, you need to march them right over here and get them to help you fix the roof, change a light, anything—just do something constructive! But no, I married the

'Marcher,' Mr. 'I-have-a dream.' Why don't you dream you had a job with some benefits so I can get the baby's teeth fixed? I had a dream, too. I dreamed I got my set of dishes off of layaway. But you're too busy going to the mountaintop. What, they wasn't hiring up there, either?"

Or what if Ghandi's wife was a nagger?

"Mahatma, get your narrow ass up off the ground! Eat some food. The neighbors are starting to talk. Come on, get up and take me out somewhere. Take me out dancing at the Flying Carpet Club. What do you mean you don't have energy? Eat some damn food. Then you'll have energy. You need protein. Look, I'm going down to McDonald's and I'm gonna get me a McCurry goat sandwich. When I come back if you don't eat, I want out of this relationship. All right fine. You don't want to eat, I want out. Here . . . take your dot back. No, no, I don't want the dot. You keep the dot. Give me the keys to the camel. I'm going downtown to find me a man who treats me as good as a cow!"

Never Big Enough

If there's one thing men think more about than they think about women, it's their penises. It's on our minds all of the time. Ladies, you have no idea how deep the obsession goes. A penis is so important that every man—whether he'll admit it or not—at one point in his life has taken a ruler or some measuring tape and measured his penis to see how much he's got. Some of us have even taken a protractor to measure the circumference.

What's worse is most men cheat with the ruler. Men lie to themselves.

Man: Hmmm . . . thirty-nine inches. That's pretty big, right? I know the ruler says three-and-a-half inches, but I've got a lot of what they call "inner shaft." My inner shaft starts up back here at the base of my neck.

And they're never big enough. Every guy wants two more inches. You think John Holmes was happy? No, he used to sit around thinking, "If I had two more inches I could tuck it in my sock." You ask a guy what the ideal size is and he'll tell you he wants it big enough to make love to a woman from another room.

The reason why we want a big dick is, basically, we want to hurt you. The biggest compliment a woman can give a guy is to roll over in the bed, holding her stomach, saying, "Damn, I think you punctured my uterus."

A man will be lying there all proud and pleased with himself, "Yeah, baby, I do that sometimes."

Let's face it, women are more mature than men. You don't see women measuring their vaginas. Well, okay, maybe it doesn't have as much to do with their maturity as a big vagina is just something a woman doesn't want to have on her résumé. It's a turn-off to guys for two reasons: It makes them feel small, and it takes too much work to please. A guy'd be whacking it, saying, "Baby, you don't feel this? How about this, are you feeling it? Nothing? Okay, let me put my leg in there. You still don't feel that? All right, let me climb in. I'm in, I am now standing inside your vagina. I'm tap dancing, break dancing, doing jumping jacks. Don't tell me you're not feeling this, either!?"

Can't Go That Long

Penis length isn't the only thing guys lie about. I had a guy tell me that he made love to his woman for six hours straight. This is impossible. First of all, you can't physically last for six hours, your back will spasm. It may feel like six hours, but I guarantee you, it's more like six minutes. And second of all, you can't apply that kind of friction to a vagina without it bursting into flames. Fellas, stop lying.

The Penis Worship Program

Women search hard for the answer to this question, "Why do men stray?" They buy self-help books, watch Oprah, and spend hours on the phone with their girlfriends just to find out how they can keep their man. Well, look no further. I have the solution to your problem. My five-step program will guarantee total satisfaction for both you and your man. After taking the Penis Worship Program you won't ever have to worry about that man straying again.

Step One

It's important that you make your man think that he has the biggest, baddest penis on the planet. Even though you both know it's not true, he needs to hear it. And you have to be the messenger. He needs to hear this morning, noon, and night, any time and any context is appropriate. For instance,

Woman: Pass me the salt, please. Do you want a piece of bread? And, oh, honey, have I ever told you that you have an incredibly fat shaft?

Step Two

Give your man plenty of head. It's not the act of giving head that turns him on, it's the fact that he's getting head that turns him on. He knows that if his girl is taking the time out of her busy day to get down on her knees and put the uncircumcised thing in her mouth she is performing one of the ultimate acts of love.

Step Three

Learn how to give a proper blow job. And get right to the point. All of that kissing on the neck and chest is unnecessary. Men don't have titties. There's no erogenous zone to be found up there. You know what a man is thinking when you start with all of that kissing? "She ain't gonna suck my dick. She's just wasting time."

Step Four

Ladies, if you don't like the way it tastes, put something on it. These are the best dipsticks ever made. Try some honey, chocolate, peanut butter, guacamole, CheezeWhiz—whatever you like. If you want to put some popcorn in the crease of his balls, he'll let you. He'll never stop you. If a man is sure that you're going to put it in your mouth, you can set it on fire and he will let you. He'll actually light it for you.

Man: All right, baby. Let's start the wienie roast. Come on, get to it! My ass hairs are burning.

Step Five

Don't make faces while giving head. It's not a sour pop. Think about how he would feel. What if your man had his head between your legs and started making faces like he's drinking wheat grass. Your feelings would be hurt, right? So, try to look like you're enjoying yourself. Maybe smile, but not a big smile 'cause you don't want him to think that you're laughing at the size of his dick. A little smirk will do.

This concludes the Penis Worship Program. If you follow the steps I guarantee that your man won't stray. HE'LL STAY!!!

Bonus

One extra tip, throw in a little choke. Men like that.

Relationship Tip #1 for Him: Keep Clean

Men, there are things that you can do to help your woman stay sexually attracted to you. Like the next time you are about to put your underwear in the hamper take the time to rub those little doo-doo stains out. Take a little soap and water and shout those out. This tells her that you're thinking about her. I mean, think about what must go through her mind when she picks up your dirty draws and sees those brown stains: "Ugh, what kind of animal am I married to? This grown man can't even wipe his ass!"

After looking at that mess how do you expect her to even consider giving you head again? It's not because she just doesn't like doing it. No. It's because she doesn't want to smell butt funk. As a preventative measure, think about buying some of those baby wipes and keep them by the bowl. A happy woman is a happy relationship!

Peany Pads

Ever notice that there are very few products for men in the drug store, but they have a whole aisle devoted to the vagina? Massengill, Monistat, Stay Free, Stay Soft, Just Stay, powders, puffs, sprays, shavers. Anything you can think of, they have for the vagina. I guess there's no market for the male organ. No soaps, no sprays, no Peany Pads, no nothing. Not even a cute little bow to tie around the shaft.

They don't have any products for the penis because it would be a hard sell. Men don't think that there's anything wrong with them. And, besides, that there's no way to sell these products on television. I mean, look at the commercials they have for women. They can suggest anything, right? You'll see two beautiful women sitting in front of a fire in a cabin on a mountaintop with snow all around them. And one of them looks over and says, "Jenny, I just don't feel fresh."

Now, we all know that what this means is, "Jenny, my vagina is stinking even up here on this mountain." But she didn't have to say that for Jenny to understand. Jenny just nods and hands over a carton of Super Absorbent Sweet Box. But see, you can't do this with a guy because guys don't understand subtlety. It'd have to be raw. Like two guys sitting on a scaffolding at a construction site eating lunch:

Jim: Hey, Tommy, my balls stink. I don't know what's wrong. I tried everything. Baby powder, talcum powder, foot spray and nothing works. It's like a freakin' laundromat down there.
Tommy: Well, Jim, have you tried Cheese-Away?
Jim: Cheese-Away, what's that?
Tommy: Cheese-Away is the first ball deodorant made especially for the hardworking blue-collar man.
Jim: Really? Can Cheese-Away help me?
Tommy: Sure, Cheese-Away helps stifle the cheese smell that occurs between the ass and the ball area. With Cheese-Away you will no longer have to deal with smelly balls. After one application your balls will smell fresh and clean. Yeah, smell that.
Jim: Minty!
Tommy: Yeah, and now Cheese-Away comes in New Car Smell.
Jim: Thanks, Cheese-Away!

Relationship Tip #2 for Her: Communication

Most women feel that men are not the best communicators. It may be that they're just not properly interpreting what their men do say. Maybe the best way for women to better understand how men communicate would be for them to listen to men when they play basketball. It's very primal. You'll see a guy coming down the court and yell at his teammate, "Motherfucka, pass the ball!"

The player handling the ball doesn't get mad, because he knows that his teammate isn't calling him a "motherfucka" per se. He knows what he's trying to say is, "Friend, we're a team here. If we're going to win this game you have to stop being selfish and share the ball."

So, the ball handler passes the basketball to his teammate, who will most likely score a basket. They share in the moment and grow closer as a result. Everybody wins.

Now, to relate this to a domestic situation, let's say a man tells his woman, "Motherfucka, bring me something to eat." She shouldn't jump to conclusions or be offended. She should take the time to understand what the man is really trying to say, which is, "Baby, when I come home from a hard day's work your food is the only thing that soothes my soul."

Women shouldn't get caught up on little words like "motherfucker." Try to understand what he's really trying to say.

Real Men Can't Talk

While men do communicate well on the basketball court, women shouldn't go thinking that men are having thoughtful, in-depth conversations with each other when they hang out. They're not. Believe me, you're not missing out on anything. Here's a typical guy conversation:

Man: Hey, man, what's up?

Other man: Nothing much. You see the ass on that girl?

Man: Yeah, I saw that. Would you hit that?

Other man: Yeah, I'd hit that. Her titties are kind of flat, though.

Man: Yeah. But I'd still hit it, though.

Other man: Yeah, I guess you're right. I'd hit it, too.

Man: All right, well, I got to get home to my woman. I'll see you later.

Other man: Yeah, me too. It was good hanging out with you.

Don't Give Him the Finger

Ladies, I don't care what you read in magazines, men don't like it when you stick your finger up their butt. It challenges their masculinity. Just because we do it to you doesn't mean we want you to reciprocate. It does not feel good. A female friend of mine was arguing with me about this. She told me, "When I put my finger in my man's ass while giving him head it makes him cum quicker." And I have to patiently explain to her, "No. He's cumming quicker because he wants you to take your finger out of his ass!"

The Condom Theory

I believe that men and women are not connecting anymore because of the condom. A lot of intimacy is getting trapped in a little plastic bubble. Men and women are going through the motions of making love, but with all of the rubber between them, emotionally they're not in tune with each other because the message the condom brings to the relationship is: I like you, but I don't trust you!

Relationship Tip #3 for Her: The Power of Lookin' Good

Women need to realize that men are visual creatures. A woman must stimulate and constantly appeal to his visual nature, otherwise, a man will lose his desire. In the beginning of the relationship women are very creative at keeping him engaged. They come to bed with a little nurse's outfit on, eight-inch pumps, saying, "I'm here to check your temperature, Big Daddy."

"You know, I was feeling a little feverish," he'll say, excited because he knows he's about to get his freak on.

But time passes in a relationship and women start to forget about his visual nature. They start coming to bed with nurse shoes on because they're comfortable. And they have that baggy army fatigue shirt on with rollers in their hair, cream on their face, and cucumbers on their eyes.

Now, if a woman who dresses like this wonders, "Why don't we make love anymore?" then she shouldn't be surprised if her man replies, "Because I'm tired of fucking the fruit stand!"

And remember there are other women out there who are dressing to seduce, constantly tempting men. Just think about fashion today. Something that was once a T-shirt is now a dress. They have a bra that can take a breast that was down by the navel and bring it up front and center. It's called a Wonder Bra because when you take it off you wonder where those nice titties went.

It's easier for women to resist temptation, because men don't dress to seduce. A guy with his shirt unbuttoned is either Arab or a faggot. I mean, when was the last time you saw a guy with one of his nuts hanging out his pants trying to be sexy, saying, "Hey, baby, how's it hanging?"

I could stand a group of women in a room and tell them what kind of panties they were wearing just at a glance: "She's wearing a G-string because there are no lines. That one has on a thong 'cause I see the little *V* in the back. Those must be period panties right there. And over here, that's laundry day."

Of course, it's unfair of a man to expect his woman to look fine all day long. Men don't understand that being a woman is really intense. A woman needs to do her hair, makeup, fingernails, toes, and eyebrows to look good, or to feel she looks good for her man. The funny thing is that all men really pay attention to is titties and ass. You'll never hear a guy say, "Man, she got a nice ass, but her eyebrows are connected. I can't get with that."

Get in Shape

Men and women need to understand why it is the relationship sometimes doesn't work out. Sometimes it's just because you are the "fat fuck" in the relationship and the other person just doesn't want to be with the "fat fuck" anymore. Let's take a look at the ladies first.

Over time women develop these big fat asses that they try to blame on child bearing or age. This is bullshit. These asses are big because they know they got their man and he's going to have to pay a lot of money to get away from their fat ass. So, they just let their ass go because they have nothing to prove. The ass can be all around the house and they don't care. You'll be saying things like, "Baby, this your ass in my shoe? Could you get it out? I gotta go to work. Could you sit on my shirt and iron it please? Thanks, Rotunda."

I haven't forgotten the men. As the years go by we develop what many call the Beer Belly, Chippy's Playground, or the Penis Obstructor. You don't have to be a beer drinker to develop this. Sometimes you get one of these bellies by simply eating too damn much. Now, while you're making love to your partner, your belly is getting all hot and sweaty from the friction, and you hear your woman screaming and you think it's because the lovin' is good but the real reason is you're giving her an Indian burn on the stomach. After it's over she has to go to the bathroom and put some cocoa butter on her belly so she can sleep. She never tells you this 'cause she loves you and doesn't want to hurt the fat fuck's feelings.

Whether you're married or single, women don't want fat, sloppy guys, so it's important to stay in shape. Women want their men on top of them, looking down, totally in control, not laying on their stomach massaging their intestines. To accomplish this, you have got to work on the upper body to develop strong arms, a strong chest and back, and a strong stomach. Forget legs, they aren't important to women or sex. Your legs can look like you have polio and it won't make a difference. It's all upper body and the ability to take your ass and touch the back of your head and then let your body thrust forward. *POW!* Now that's a stroke.

I went to a twenty-four-hour gym in Hollywood, which was really strange. Seems like the later you go, the weirder the people get. There was a dude that hung in the showers. He didn't work out, he just hung in the showers washing his belly, like he's thinking, "Yummy, look at all this dick. Hmm, hmm." I can't wash up there. I just go home stinking. Besides, I'm lifting light weights so I don't really work up a sweat. I'm trying to get toned, not buff. That's the excuse guys use when they can't lift heavy weights. After I do about six curls, I go to the mirror for about half an hour of flexing.

"Yeah, this is coming along. I'm looking good, Jack," I'd say, smashing my arm against my ribs to try and make my bicep look bigger.

And I feel good until one of those musclebound cats comes along and lets me know just how big I am. "Excuse me, little man, can I get to those three hundreds?"

Truthfully I never go above one hundred pounds because once I tried to bench press one hundred and twenty and the bar got stuck on me. Have you ever lifted weights and you get trapped on the bench? I had done about twenty-five presses. When I tried to push it back up, the shit got real heavy. My hands started trembling and I couldn't get it off me. I was too embarrassed to ask for help. So, I'm laying there, struggling, making little bitch noises until finally the dude in the bathroom comes running out, rubbing his stomach, yelling, "What's going on out here? Is somebody lifting a hundred pounds? Oooh, let me help you, you poor thing!"

On Impact

You know who I feel sorry for? The guy who thinks he's gay and then finds out that he's not—on impact. I wonder what goes through a guy's mind before he takes that step, because you don't just up and do that. You have to meditate on it because it's not like golf, you can't buy a mulligan. There is no do-over. I can just see a guy sitting around thinking:

Steve: I wonder what's wrong with me. I'm not attracted to women anymore. I find football to be very violent and actually think ice skating is beautiful. Maybe I'm gay. Yeah. Maybe I need to explore that side. But what should I do? Where should I go? . . . Oh, wait! *(retrieves a slip of paper from his pants pocket)* Maybe I'll call Bob. Bob is gay. He can help me.

So, he picks up the phone and dials.

Steve: Hello, Bob?
Bob: Who's this?
Steve: You don't know me, but my name is Steve. I got your name off of a bathroom wall. It said, "For a good time call Bob."
Bob: I was drunk out of my mind when I wrote that. But, yes, I've been known to be a party animal. So, what can I do for you, stranger?

Steve: Well, I think I'm gay, and I don't know what to do.
Bob: Oh, you poor baby. I'll be right over.

Click. Bob hangs up. Now Steve is probably having second thoughts.

Steve: Oh my God, what have I done? Bob's coming over and I don't have a thing to wear. Look at this place, I better straighten up. Put on the TV. Oh, look, Scott Hamilton, this is perfect.

Ding Dong. The doorbell rings. Steve is afraid to open the door. *Ding Dong.*

Steve: How the hell did he get here so fast?

Ding Dong. Knock, knock, knock.

Bob: Steve, open up. It's me, Bob! Listen, I know you're afraid and you're probably having second thoughts. I know, because I was there once. Just relax. Everything is gonna be okay. You have to trust me.

Steve takes a deep breath and finally opens the door.

Steve: Thanks for coming over. I want you to know that I'm not sure about this, so I don't want to rush anything.
Bob: I'm here for you, Stevie. All I want is for you to feel safe. That's the only thing that's important to me, okay? Now, let's smoke a joint, it'll relax you.

Steve: Wow, this is some good stuff.

Bob: Only the best for you. I got it from this really cute drug dealer. Now, come sit on my lap and tell me who the fish was that broke your heart.

Steve: Do I have to sit on your lap?

Bob: Yes, it's the rules. Here, have a shot of tequila. It'll help to relax you.

Steve sits on his lap.

Steve: Well, there was this girl, Bob.

Bob: I knew it, that bitch! What did she do to you?

Steve: She told me I was a freak because I wanted to have anal sex. She said it was nasty and perverted.

Bob: You poor baby. Keep smokin'.

Steve: Then she said that I wasn't man enough to be in a relationship with her 'cause I was too close to my mother, and I was sexually abused by my father, all I know is . . .

Bob: Time's up.

Steve: I was just getting to the deep part.

Bob: Honey, I don't have all day. Look, I want to officially welcome you to the other side. You're now gay. Drink up.

Steve: That's it? Just like that?

Bob: Sweetie, any man that can sit on another man's lap, drunk, and talk about being sodomized by his father is a fag. All we need to do is seal it. I'm gonna need you to sign this consent slip to protect both of us in case of a lawsuit. I got into this very ugly little episode with this really cute Asian boy named Hung-low. Okay, I'm ready if you are. Would you like another sip of tequila before we get started? No? Okay, let's do it.

Steve: OH GOD, PLEASE STOP! YOU'RE HURTING ME! PLEASE STOP THIS! I DON'T LIKE IT! YOU'RE HURTING ME!

Bob: Just hold on, honey. It's almost over. Isn't this what you wanted to do to your girlfriend?

The Gay Way

Statistics show that more and more people are turning gay, especially women. Which makes sense when you think about how convenient it would be to have a relationship where two people have everything in common. Take two women, for instance. They can go to Bed Bath & Beyond all day long and play with little soaps, feel up the fabrics, and sniff candles. There's no one there to say, "Can we get the hell out of here, or is there an electronics department in this place?"

After all the shopping is done they can hold hands, skip home, and talk about nothing for the rest of the afternoon. Then, they can eat each other out and still have enough energy to talk about nothing some more. No stress, no problems.

Gay men have it easy, too. They don't have to worry about feelings. "Did I satisfy him?" is a question that will never have to enter his mind because it doesn't take much to satisfy a guy. You can even have sex and watch the game at the same time. The other man will never look up and say "Are you watching the Lakers, or are you watching me?"

Relationship Tip #4 for Her: Insensitivity and Men

Women should not take men's lack of sensitivity personally. Understanding that they are incapable of being considerate and saying the right thing at the right time will make a woman's life much easier and enjoyable.

Men are taught at a young age how not to "feel." A little boy can get hit in the face with a baseball bat and the first thing his friend will say is, "Man, stop acting like a bitch. Be a man. Pick your teeth up . . . here's your eye. Come on and let's finish the game."

A woman who asks for honesty from her man should be wary. If a man really tries to be honest with his woman he will inevitably end up hurting her feelings. Let's see, for instance, what happens when a woman asks her husband if he thinks she's put on a little weight.

Woman: God, this skirt doesn't fit me anymore. Honey, do you think I'm getting fat?

Men: Well . . .

Woman: Now be honest.

Man: Be honest? Well, okay baby, your ass is getting a little too wide there. Lately I feel like I've been sleeping with Al Sharpton. What? Why you crying?

So Romantic

Things that are romantic to women are bull-shit to men. Women like to take long walks on the beach, long walks in the park. They say things like,

Woman: Oh, it's such a beautiful night for a stroll. Look at the stars. See how there're twinkling and bright.

Meanwhile, the man is thinking to himself.

Man: I've seen better stars while you were blowing me. Let's go back home, my feet hurt.

Reality Check

If you ask a woman what she wants in a man, the list is way too long. It's like a grocery list. Here's a woman shopping for a man: "He's got to have a good job, a nice car, money in the bank, and good credit; he's got to be athletic, a nice dresser, have good hair and a sexy smile; he's got to be a tender lover, with a great sense of humor, and he's got to be good with children."

Look, ladies, Michael Jordan is taken. So, come down to earth and get one of the humans. And be happy if you get "good job and good dick" out of the deal.

Still Standing

Viagra is supposed to generate over a billion dollars revenue in one year and the FDA hasn't fully tested it yet. That means it must've gotten one guy really hard and they just started selling it: "Listen guy, you want some of this shit or what? I'm telling you it works. Go ahead slam the door on it. . . . See, still hard, still standing. . . . What, you want some more proof? Okay, go ahead throw the baseball. You see that? I gave some to Mark McGwire and he went and hit all those home runs. No, it didn't have anything to do with those muscle supplements. Okay, one more demonstration. Okay, go ahead. Change your tire. Take your time this thing ain't going nowhere."

Thank You, Viagra

I have an idea for a Viagra commercial:
A man stands in the back of an elevator. He has packages in both arms.

Then a beautiful woman enters the elevator. She has packages in both of her arms, too. She is struggling to press her button but can't quite get to it.

The man watches her with a smug look on his face.

Man: Don't worry, ma'am, I'll get that for you. Please stand back.

She stands aside. He thrusts his hips forward and presses the button. *DING!*

Woman: *(stunned and impressed)* Why, thank you!

Man turns to the camera and winks.

Man: No, thank Viagra.

Relationship Tip #5 for Her: The Power of Indifference

Women need to learn to use indifference. It's a word that they hate because they feel it means you don't care. That's not true. Indifference is how men control women because they do care, they just don't show it. Here's how women can apply indifference in their relationships. Say you want to go out with your man.

Woman: Baby, can we go out tonight?
Man: Naw, I ain't feelin' it. I just want to stay home and watch some TV.

Do not get all emotional and start crying and throwing things at him.

Woman: You bastard! You never want to take me anywhere! I feel like a prisoner! All you want to do is watch your damn football!

This only helps him justify not taking you anywhere.

Man: See, that's why I don't take you out 'cause we'll get to the club and you're going to start this silly shit up in there and I'm going to have to knock you upside your damn head.

Ladies, what you want to do is apply indifference. Control your emotions and simply say the following:

Woman: Okay, honey. If that's what you want to do, I'll just go hang out with the girls. We'll go down to the Coconut Teaser. Here, let me fix you something to eat and get you some beer, and you have a great time, okay?

Then, you go in the room and put on your little "ho" outfit. You want to take your panties off and put them in your pocketbook. Then, while he's watching TV you bend over and turn down the volume, making sure you give him a little peek at your other smile.

Woman: Bye, honey.

As soon as you walk out that door, he's going to say:

Man: Bye, honey, my ass.

I guarantee you that your man will be at the Coconut Teaser. He may be in a disguise, but he will be there.

Same thing applies to sex. If you're lying in your bed and you want to have sex with your man and he says:

Man: Naw, baby, I gotta get up early tomorrow. I'm tired.

Don't get mad. Control those emotions. Remember this: A man always wants to have sex. If he says, "I'm tired," it really means, "Do something freaky for me, 'cause I'm tired of you on your back like a roach." So, what you want to do is get up, go in the other room, put on some porno, and start playing with yourself. Make noise to let him know what you're doing, and a few minutes later you'll look up and see him standing in the doorway jerking off. I guarantee you will be having sex that night. That's how you apply indifference.

Don't Fake Your Orgasms

Why do women fake orgasms? They shouldn't do that. Don't do that to the man and don't do it to yourself, because you make that man who's just lying on your stomach, moving his head, think that he's doing something. If you let him get away with bad sex, he's never gonna try any harder to please you. This is what you wanna do. If you want a man to please you, just lay there and don't say anything—just lie down and start whistling, make phone calls.

Woman: Hi, Mom. Ah, I'm not doing anything, just waiting for my nails to dry.

See that will mess with his ego and then he'll start working, 'cause he's gonna want your attention.

Man: Oh no, you gonna put the phone down, you gonna put that damn phone down now.

Too bad men can't fake orgasms. It would be the ultimate power. The problem is we leave evidence. You can't be sitting there in the wet spot, saying, "I was just faking . . . and now I'm gonna pretend to be really, really tired."

Love Noise

Ladies, don't ever think that you can lay on your back while your man is making love to you and not make any noise. That's damaging to his ego. Now if you don't care about the man, by all means continue being quiet. In fact, if you want him out of your life, file your nails while you're fucking him. But if you love this man and want to make him feel like a man, make some noise!

You're supposed to be his cheerleader. Sing opera if you have to. Don't be afraid to wake up the neighbor because the neighbor will come to respect your man. He'll see him out in the street and give him the thumbs-up sign.

Neighbor: Good morning, Mr. Wilson. I heard y'all last night. Just want to say thank you. I jerked off to y'all.

The best-case scenario would be if the cops showed up. This would boost his ego in ways you can't imagine. Your man would have to go to the door with a towel around his waist and explain what happened. There'd be a S.W.A.T. team outside, an army of police cruisers and helicopters playing their spotlights all over the neighborhood.

Man: Hey, what's happenin', officer?

Police: Well, we have some complaints of a possible murder.

Man: No, it wasn't no murder. . . . I was killing some pussy though. . . . Ha Ha Ha. I do that sometimes.

Police: Well, you're gonna have to keep it down.

Man: I can't, it's the Viagra. You wanna see what caused all of the ruckus? *(drops the towel)* Go ahead, hit it with your billy club, it ain't going anywhere. That's Viagra. Matter of fact, you can shoot it and it will stay hard.

Finding the Touch Again

Did you hear about the eighty-year-old man that left his wife and got a younger woman after taking Viagra? I can't say I really blame him. It's probably been fifteen years since the poor old man has had an erection, and I'm sure after sixty years of nagging she had something to do with his dysfunction.

He finally gets it up and he's thinking, "Man, do I have to use it on this eighty-year-old woman? She wears an oxygen mask and a heart monitor. How can I have sex with that?"

Hell, he'd have to use defibrillators just to get her wet. "Okay, give me four hundred volts, stat. Clear!" And you know his wife would try to doll herself up. But it wouldn't work. Imagine her in some Victoria Secrets on a walker, saying things like, "Taste my diaper. It's edible."

The old guy would have to help her to the bed and onto all fours with her breasts dripping down. She'd say, "Okay, Daddy, I want you to knock my teeth out from the back. What are you waiting on? Stop being silly, it's just a hemorrhoid."

Man, that's just nasty. Maybe they ought to screen people before they actually prescribe the Viagra. What's an eighty-year-old man doing having sex anyway?

Relationship Tip #6 for Him: Women Can't Mind Their Business

When a man comes home from work, he wants quiet, just to be left alone for a while. Women, however, can't resist trying to pry their way into his head by saying things like, "What are you thinking?"

Of course, a man would just get angry and say something to upset her, such as, "I'm thinking, can I kill you and get away with it?"

This is simply not going to work if you want a meaningful and productive relationship. Men need to learn the female language, to look behind the veneer at what is really going on in a woman's head. It has taken me years to figure out that when a woman asks you that question they just want some attention. That in mind, see how successful the following approach is:

Woman: What are you thinking?
Man: Why, I'm thinking about you, dear.
Woman: Oh, that's so sweet. Okay, well, I'm going to leave you alone because I know you must have a lot on your mind.

Women Know!

Men, I don't care how slick you might think you are, women can tell when you are cheating on them. They've got some special radar, their powers of intuition.

Wife: I had a bad dream last night.
Husband: What about?
Wife: I dreamed there was a snake in my bed.
Husband: Are you serioussss? That soundsss like a ssscary, ssscary story. I need sssome lotion, my ssskin is ssstaring to ssshed.

Just Sex

When you have an affair there's always the chance that the other women will start to develop strong feelings for you. Before you know it this woman that agreed that the relationship would be strictly sexual will utter the words like:

Woman: Are you going home to her?
Man: Yes. If it wasn't for her I wouldn't be here.

Female Friends

You can't be friends with a fine woman, otherwise, you're going to want to sleep with her. If you need a female friend, find you a big, fat, ugly woman. They're the best friends, except there is a whole lot of emotional baggage you have to deal with. You being the friend are the one that has to talk her fat ass off the roof every week: "Come down, Rotunda, you're not that fat. Come on, let's go get some ice cream and Twinkies. I'll pay. Come on, there's an all-you-can-eat down at Sizzler. See, I knew you'd come down, buddy."

It's All in the Mind

I used to play this mind game on myself whenever I saw a pretty woman that tempted me. What I would do is look at this woman and find a physical flaw, then I would animate her flaw in my mind until it turned me off. Like, a pair of little legs in my mind would look like pool sticks. This worked for years without any problems. Until I moved to LA. Some women in LA are flawless. I'd run across women who were so beautiful, I'd have a problem finding anything wrong, so I had to make some adjustments in my mind. I had to start thinking about what's wrong on the inside. "She probably has a cyst on her ovaries. Her intestines are probably all backed up with red meat. I bet she wipes to the front."

Relationship Tip for Her #7: No Farting

When a man is in love with you, he puts you on a pedestal. You are his queen, his baby, his boo. You are the one he brags to his friends about at work and there is only one person in this world that can knock you off of this pedestal. And that person is you.

How? you might wonder. By farting. Don't ever fart around your man! It ruins his image of you as his flower. You become a stink weed. How is your man supposed to keep you on that pedestal when you're farting around him? I guess you might say, "Well, he does it."

Yes, he does, but he also pees standing up. Are you going to try that, too? Men are pigs. He's supposed to fart. He's farting for the both of you, which is why it smells so bad. Just because your man is nasty it doesn't mean he's trying to get into a farting contest with you. You start pootin' around your man, he's gonna stop doing all the nice things that he used to do for you, like holding the door open, because now he's thinking, "I'm gonna hold this door for this bitch, and then she's gonna go and fart. And I'm gonna have to walk behind her and smell it? You get the door your damned self!"

Women v. Women

Woman are very strange creatures. Most don't like to see other women happy. Whether it's envy or jealousy, I don't know, but I'd be hanging out with a woman and if a pretty woman walks by, the first thing that comes out of her mouth is, "That bitch thinks she's cute."

Men don't trip like that. You'll never see man look at another man and say, "He thinks he's got a nice ass." A man knows he shouldn't be looking at this guy's ass in the first place.

Save the World with a Dick

Men, too, are strange in their own way. Every man thinks that the key to any problem on earth is "some good dick"! A guy will look at a lesbian and say, "All that ho needs is some good dick." They can look at a cancer patient and say, "To hell with chemo. All she needs is some good dick and she'll be up and around in no time." They can even be in a morgue, saying, "So what she's dead? Some good dick'll resurrect that ho."

A Female President

I would love to see a female president in my lifetime. It would be a huge step for women and prove how far we've come as a society. Women are as capable as men, and if they run households and companies, they can run a country. And they can't mess things up any more than men have over the past few centuries. But, really, I don't think a woman will become president anytime soon. They are just too emotional. A man can separate logic from his emotions. Like, at a time of war a male president can address the nation by simply saying, "We are at war." It's a direct statement of fact with no touchy-feely stuff.

I don't think a women can be that cold. Her declaration would go something like this: "Hello, friends. I'm sorry to interrupt your evening, but I regret to have to inform you that we're having a little spat with our friends in Iraq. Remember when I invited Mr. Hussein and his wife over for supper? Well, I made lobster Newburg with a lovely white wine sauce with a three bean salad because I'm on a diet right now. Anyway, everything was hunky-dory until I looked down and saw that that bitch had the nerve to be wearing the same shoes as me. Oh no, she knew I was gonna wear them and she wore hers anyway. Then the ho started flirting with my man right in front of me. Uh-uh, I'm not having that. We are at war. It's on!"

Acknowledgments

Many thanks to David Asbery, Stephen Barnes, Annice Parker, David M. Schnaid, La Trenda Carey, Toni Phillips, Ann Develin Blanchard, Dan Strone, the William Morris Agency, Mauro DiPreta, Toisan Craigg, David Hirshey, NY Comic Strip Live, Improvisation (LA), Comedy Store, the entire east coast and west coast Way-Tang Clan—*where black unity still exists*, and **special thanks** to the loves of my life; my source of inspiration (and jokes), my wife and kids—Lisa, Damon, Michael, Cara Mia, and Kyla.